ADVANCE PRAISE FOR *BLISS MORE*

"Light Watkins's approach to meditation is both simple and profound. With him as your guide, you will unlock the secrets to establishing a regular and powerfully healthy daily practice."
—Deepak Chopra, M.D., co-author of *The Healing Self*

"This lovely book could very well be the life-changer you've been looking for. It sweeps away stigmas and dogmatism and rigidities, and plunks you down right where you are, with all you need to grow and evolve and become ever more yourself. It's easy to read, and it's also easy to put into practice. If you've ever wondered if meditating might enrich your life, this book could very well hold the key you need to succeed."
—John Robbins, author of *The New Good Life* and president of Food Revolution Network

"Light's approach to meditation is as easy as you'll find in any book, and his years of expertise are apparent in the way he simplifies the process so the everyman can start meditating with success right away."
—Jason Wachob, founder and CEO of mindbodygreen and author of *Wellth*

"Light is the modern-day meditation master who doesn't live in the mountains. He shows us a simple way to find inner calm during chaos. Tap into this book now!"
—Lewis Howes, author of *The School of Greatness*

"Light was my meditation teacher, and *Bliss More* perfectly encapsulates the timeless wisdom I learned in his training. If you're ready to start a solid meditation practice, look no further."
—Rosario Dawson, actress

"It's impossible to read *Bliss More* and not come away with a comprehensive understanding of how easy and simple meditation can be, why you should be practicing it daily, and how it will improve your life in meaningful and transformative ways."
—Mark Hyman, M.D., author of *Eat Fat, Get Thin* and *The Blood Sugar Solution*

"Light saved my life! Take it from a nebbishy, neurotic, anxious comedian who used to hyperventilate his way through life—meditation saved me, and Light showed me the way!"
—Eric Andre, comedian, *The Eric Andre Show*

"Light Watkins is a gentle, generous, brilliant teacher and a masterful translator of timeless wisdom. *Bliss More* is not only a book that's fun to read; but while you're in that sweet cradle of Light's engaging storytelling, you'll effortlessly absorb the tools and techniques to cultivate a lifelong meditation practice. *Bliss More* is a treasure trove of powerful, practical, and priceless techniques to finally master your meditation practice."

—davidji, meditation teacher and author of *Sacred Powers*

"Light Watkins is a postmodern mix of deep practitioner, lighthearted teacher, incredible community builder, and skilled writer and artist. His work is much needed on the planet right now."

—Guru Jagat, founder of RA MA Yoga
and author of *Invincible Living*

"In *Bliss More*, Light Watkins has decoded the art of meditation by crafting an accessible, user-friendly, step-by-step manual to becoming an expert meditator and finding your inner bliss. This book is fitting for everyone—from novices to experts!"

—Agapi Stassinopoulos, author of *Wake Up to the Joy of You*

"With *Bliss More*, Light has created the go-to book for learning how to meditate with ease. He includes nuggets of wisdom that will improve the experience of every kind of meditator—from the newbie to the skeptic to the seasoned practitioner."

—Michael Dubin, founder of Dollar Shave Club

"In *Bliss More*, Light masterfully debunks my long-held belief as a fellow meditation teacher that meditation can't be effectively 'taught' in a book. The journey he takes you on is natural and evolves into increasing depth. Best of all, it effortlessly applies to modern life. The technique shared will stay with you for a lifetime, as will the wisdom found within Light's personal stories and anecdotes."

—Megan Monahan, meditation teacher

"In a confusing world of information, one fact always comes up undisputed—meditating is good for you. I was 'too busy' and 'didn't know how' to meditate. Light Watkins has been the individual to show me just how easy it is to make meditation a part of my everyday life. We all owe those few minutes a day to ourselves."

—Gabby Reece, professional volleyball player and
author of *My Foot Is Too Big for the Glass Slipper*

"I recommend that all of my patients start a meditation practice, and while it's ideal to learn with a teacher, *Bliss More* is one of the best meditation books I've ever come across for getting you started. Light has the gift of being able to demystify meditation in a way that will make you want to meditate, even if you feel your mind is too busy."

—Frank Lipman, M.D., author of *10 Reasons You Feel Old and Get Fat*

"Light Watkins is an extremely knowledgeable Vedic teacher. In this beautifully written how-to guide, he takes the essence of that tradition and makes it accessible, perhaps for the first time ever in written form. Utilizing the E.A.S.Y. technique he gives you everything you need to know to launch a practice that relieves deep-rooted stress and helps you live a more meaningful life."

—Lodro Rinzler, author of *The Buddha Walks into a Bar . . .* and co-founder of MNDFL

"Light is a quintessential teacher. He not only shows us why we should be meditating daily, but how to do so in a way that just makes common sense. The personal stories and real-world testimonials from his meditation students will make you excited about sitting with your eyes closed each day."

—Leon Logothetis, author of *The Kindness Diaries*

"There is no one more effective at teaching the new generation of meditators than Light Watkins. You'll find his smart, no-nonsense, story-driven approach extremely refreshing and inspiring."

—Jesse Israel, founder of The Big Quiet

"My mind is a hairball of crazy thoughts most the time. If it wasn't for meditation and gratitude and all the groovy things Light Watkins teaches, my picture might have ended up at the post office instead of on the back cover of my nineteen books. And that's why I am so excited about the book you're holding in your hands. Light takes the world's most powerful practice and turns it into something you can't wait to do. Something you're actually excited about. As I always say, if it's not fun, it's not sustainable. With this book, Light makes meditation fun, sustainable, and ridiculously easy. Take that, monkey mind."

—Pam Grout, author of *E-Squared, Thank & Grow Rich,* and *Art & Soul, Reloaded*

BY LIGHT WATKINS

Bliss More
The Inner Gym

BLISS
MORE

How to Succeed in Meditation
Without Really Trying

LIGHT WATKINS

BALLANTINE BOOKS

New York

4168

No book can replace the diagnostic expertise and medical advice of a trusted physician. Please be certain to consult with your doctor before making any decisions that affect your health, particularly if you suffer from any medical condition or have any symptom that may require treatment.

This is a work of nonfiction. Some names and identifying details have been changed.

Published in the United States by Ballantine Books, an imprint of Random House, a division of Penguin Random House LLC, New York.

BALLANTINE and the HOUSE colophon are registered trademarks of Penguin Random House LLC.

LIBRARY OF CONGRESS CATALOGING-IN-PUBLICATION DATA
Names: Watkins, Light, author.
Title: Bliss more : how to succeed in meditation without really trying / Light Watkins.
Description: New York : Ballantine Books, 2018. | Includes index.
Identifiers: LCCN 2017042651 | ISBN 9780399180354 (hardcover : alk. paper) | ISBN 9780399180361 (ebook)
Subjects: LCSH: Meditation. | Medicine and psychology. | Health.
Classification: LCC BL627 .W375 2018 | DDC 158.1/2—dc23
LC record available at https://lccn.loc.gov/2017042651

Printed in the United States of America on acid-free paper

randomhousebooks.com

2 4 6 8 9 7 5 3 1

First Edition

Designed by Debbie Glasserman

This book is dedicated to all seekers.
Without the spiritually curious, there would
be no such thing as meditation.

All of humanity's problems
stem from man's inability
to sit quietly in a room alone.

—*Blaise Pascal*

CONTENTS

INTRODUCTION

It's Time

It's very hard.

I don't have time.

I'm not in the mood.

I don't really need it.

I do it only when I need to, but on my own terms.

I can't sit still for very long.

I like the idea of it more than the act of it.

My meditation is drawing.

My mind is too busy.

These are all common excuses I've used in the past for not enjoying a regular, daily, seated meditation practice. Do any of them sound familiar?

My involvement in meditation dates back nearly twenty years, but I will tell you up front that the overwhelming majority of my initial efforts were, at best, mediocre and, at worst, an exercise in futility—and by *initial* I'm referring to the first few *years* of dabbling.

I first got the idea to try meditating while in yoga classes, where my teachers mentioned that the sole purpose of doing yoga was to prepare our bodies for seated meditation. The various spiritual books I was reading at the time also echoed the importance of meditation as a path to experiencing inner bliss, or nirvana, an internal experience reportedly so serene that you would lose awareness of all of your worries, doubts, and fears and be bathed in a feeling of oneness. Who could resist such a promise? I didn't need any more convincing that meditation would do me a world of good, but I was skeptical about my ability to get my mind to the needed place.

I lived in New York at the time and found a weekly class (the cost was a five-dollar donation) held in the bell tower of the historic Riverside Church, close to my apartment. Martha, the facilitator, started off by telling us about her meditation master, a professional snowboarder and music producer who gained enlightenment on a snowy mountaintop in Nepal after a miraculous run-in with a Buddhist monk. He taught meditation and spirituality for many years and died in his forties (Martha was vague about his cause of death, which I discovered later was suicide), leaving behind an archive of New Age music he produced, to which his students began meditating.

Martha instructed us to sit up tall (with our backs erect, not touching the chair), close our eyes, and give our full attention to one of the songs that was composed by the aforementioned meditation master. While listening, she encouraged us to feel the sensations in our body and mind, and be present to the sounds and vibrations within the song. If our mind got distracted and began veering off to some errant thought, we were to let go of the thought and return our attention to the New Age music, which sounded like a mash-up of smooth jazz and opera. This was not what I was expecting. But I sat there trying to remain open to the possibility of having the intended meditative experience. Maybe the monk would appear to me in my meditation, I thought—half sarcastically and half optimistically.

Four minutes in, I felt nothing but frustration. When the song ended, Martha had us open our eyes and share our experiences. One woman reported hearing the subtle sounds embedded within the song. The guy next to me said he felt a delightful tingly sensation in his hands and feet. Others reported similar experiences of movement of energy, or celestial epiphanies. I kept quiet, because the entire time I felt like I had been just sitting there, listening to New Age music with my eyes closed.

We "meditated" through three or four more songs that first night, and although I desperately wanted to intuit some hidden message about the universe—or simply just feel *anything*—nothing special happened. Maybe I was trying too hard, I thought. Or perhaps I needed to come back and give it another try next week. Maybe it would take another three months . . .

Disappointed, I dropped my five-dollar bill into the donation bucket on the way out and rode my bike home, not fully sure if I would ever crack the elusive meditation code. Being as curious as I was skeptical, though, I vowed to return to Martha's group, even if it meant remaining insecure about my inability to silence my mind and feel the supposed bliss of meditation.

I took personal responsibility for my lack of success. Could it have been all the fast food and soda pop I consumed while growing up in Alabama? Was it possible I had a genetic mental block that prohibited me from achieving the elusive state of bliss? Could it be that I was already enlightened and didn't need to meditate at all?

Nah. Turns out I just went to the wrong class.

Unfortunately, it would take another couple of years of dabbling in different meditation scenes before I figured that out. In the meantime, the novelty of telling people that I meditated was enough to keep me curious about the practice. They didn't have to know that I wasn't actually experiencing anything in meditation other than my normal thinking mind. In fact, nobody had to know.

HOW NOT TO MEDITATE

I heard several of my yoga teachers insist that there is no "right" way to meditate—that we are our own guru, and therefore we should do what feels right to us in the moment. Therefore, I constantly wondered if I was practicing the best style for me.

At various times in those early years, I tried meditating with my back straight and legs crossed, as I had seen monks do in movies. I tried meditating while lying down, meditating in a field of grass, meditating at the end of yoga class, meditating while sitting on a yoga bolster, meditating on my friend's living room floor. I tried astral-traveling meditations, channeling meditations, communing-with-my-spirit-guide meditations, Zen meditations, mindfulness meditations, barefoot-walking meditations, holotropic-breathing meditations, mala-bead meditations, and staring-at-the-candle meditations, as well as frequent meditation sits at the local Hare Krishna temple.

Gradually, it dawned on me that if meditation delivers a blissful experience, it must happen about as often as Halley's Comet appears in the night sky. By far the more common experience I had was physical pain from sitting with my back straight, interspersed with the frustration of battling my mind, chased with heavy doses of boredom.

Over time, my default position became sitting with my legs crossed, with my back as straight as possible, while resting my palms on my thighs, and with my thumb and index fingers lightly touching. But time and again, instead of feeling my chakras align, or my energy shift—or *anything,* for that matter—mostly what I felt was searing pain in my lower back while my bare ankles dug into the hard floor so that I could keep pressing my back into a more upright position. Meanwhile, my erratic mind played variations of good-cop-bad-cop, bad-cop-bad-cop, and bad-cop-worse-cop when it came to my ability to meditate with success, which often left me checking my watch every thirty seconds and counting down the minutes until the dreaded experience was over.

I was becoming increasingly discouraged and jaded. Why were people so enthusiastic about this spiritual torture experience? How could something so obviously laborious continue to exist for thousands of years? How did the word "bliss" ever come to be associated with such a thoroughly unblissful experience? I felt like I was living in some sort of bizarre meditation version of *The Emperor's New Clothes*—standing on the sidelines as the procession went by, witnessing everyone else sing the praises of this glorious practice that was supposedly garbed in pure bliss.

Ironically, when I became a yoga teacher a few years after my inaugural meditation experience in New York, I began leading guided meditations at the end of my classes. I was seen as a meditation expert even though I never received meditation instruction during my yoga teacher training, nor did I have a consistent meditation practice of my own at the time. In order to compensate for my personal inability to sit in silence, I did what many yoga teachers do, and parroted the stock meditation instructions I heard *my* yoga teachers give over the years: let go of your worries, visualize waterfalls and white lights enveloping you, calm your mind, and don't forget to notice your breath in the process. In other words, I became the emperor!

Nobody needed to know how much of a monkey mind I was experiencing while I was guiding them, or how much I struggled to feel my own bliss. I knew how to look and sound the part, soft voice and all. Maybe that's the jig, I thought: *everyone* is pretending, and meditation is all about faking like you're blissed out even though you aren't.

What I didn't know then, and probably wouldn't have believed if someone had told me, was that I was about to experience a 180-degree turn in my attitude toward meditation. Indeed, meditation would soon become the bliss-inducing practice I had always hoped it could be, and would revolutionize my life in the most unexpected ways.

WHEN THE STUDENT IS READY

In 2003, I relocated to Los Angeles and befriended a yoga teacher named Will, who shared my interest in spiritual studies.

Will also loved to meditate—a lot. It didn't matter what we were about to do: go for a run, check out a movie, head to lunch. If we spent more than a few hours together, Will would inevitably pop the dreaded question: "Hey, you want to meditate?"

I liked that Will was so enthusiastic about meditation, but I hated the fact that it meant I had to endure another fifteen or twenty minutes of torture while waiting for him to be done. I would often glance over at him from my meditation seat, and while I was battling my mind, his slight smile hinted that he was having a far more positive experience. His pleasant demeanor was effortless, like that of a baby enjoying a sweet dream. I had no idea what Will knew that I didn't, but if it wasn't for his example, I probably would've given up on meditating.

One day while at lunch, Will mentioned a meditation teacher he had studied with ten years before. He spoke about this person with such familiarity and adoration, almost like he was referring to a close relative. I was surprised that he was just now mentioning him, after all the time we'd spent together meditating.

Shortly after, Will announced that his meditation teacher was coming to town to give a talk on meditation, and he invited me to join him. I was curious to meet this person that my good friend so admired—but less intrigued about learning how to meditate from yet another teacher suggesting I needed to let go of my worries and sit up straighter. As far as I was concerned, I was already experienced in those approaches, well beyond the need for instruction, because I'd already been teaching it to others. I knew the language. I was relatively calm, so what could this person teach someone like me? Surely he was coming to speak with people who knew nothing about meditation and had zero experience with the practice.

I turned up that night at Will's apartment and took a seat on the living room floor, assuming my usual straight-backed, cross-legged meditation position. Once everyone was settled, Will welcomed his master meditation teacher into the room. A moment later, the teacher emerged from the back of the apartment, glided through the crowd of about thirty people, and sat comfortably in the wide and sturdy antique wooden chair that had been placed in the front of the crowd. He introduced himself (we'll refer to him as MV) and, with a playful smile, MV asked if everyone was happy.

When you hear someone introduced as a "master meditation guru," you think of someone of Indian descent, someone maybe wearing a robe or with a longish gray beard. You think of a person with mala beads dripping from their neck and wrists. You think of someone with a foreign accent. But MV the meditation guru had none of those things.

In fact, he was dressed more like an insurance salesman, with khakis, a button-down shirt, and a blazer. He was tanned, middle-aged, slightly balding, and clean-shaven—no accent, beard, or beads. However, he had a glow and a presence that suggested he knew things. And strangely, within about ten minutes of being in his presence, I felt a deep calling to learn as much as I could from him.

This man and everything about his presence redefined bliss in my eyes. I assumed that bliss was something that you felt only *in* meditation. But watching my future teacher that first night made me realize that I had bliss all wrong. Bliss is more about what you experience and exude *outside* of meditation, in your life. It's a state of being that can be felt by others the moment you enter a room. I wanted to experience that level of bliss for myself. I wanted to have that same effect on others. And I concluded in that moment that I was meant to teach people how to attain it for themselves.

HOW I LEARNED TO SUCCEED IN MEDITATION

Now that I was clear about my new purpose in life, and even had a role model to help guide me, I set out to learn what I could from him.

With MV as my guide, over the next few days of comprehensive meditation training I discovered that the reason I had so many clunky meditation experiences in the past was that I had been using *too much* effort, both physically and mentally. Instead of allowing meditation to work for me, as designed, I had been working hard to quiet my mind. MV taught me how to do less in meditation and accomplish more than I ever thought possible. And eventually, like Will, I finally knew what a settled mind felt like. I understood why it was happening, and I knew exactly what I needed to do in order to "allow" it to happen again. And again. And again. It was amazing—I had no clue that meditation could be so accessible, so deep, and feel so good!

Inspired by my good fortune, I began shadowing MV, helping him whenever he taught new groups of meditators, and in the process I learned more about his guru, who did fit the stereotype of the Indian man with the beard, the robe, and the beads—Maharishi Mahesh Yogi, the founder of Transcendental Meditation. MV told countless stories about his experiences with Maharishi and the Indian tradition from which Transcendental Meditation originated. I went on to study ancient Indian philosophy, and another year or two later I was invited to accompany MV and some of his other protégés to northern India to learn how to teach meditation in the same way that he had been taught by his teacher.

We converged upon a hamlet nestled in the foothills of the Himalayas called Rishikesh, about a day and a half by car from the source of the sacred Ganges River, and we began our immersive instruction to become master meditation teachers. About three months and over a thousand hours of meditation later, I completed my training and returned to Los Angeles as a newly minted Vedic meditation teacher. I was excited to pay it forward and show my friends, other yogis, and really anyone who wanted to learn how to meditate with ease and tap into their bliss—basically, everyone's goal in meditation, and quite the opposite of my first few years of do-it-yourself attempts.

I found the simple, structured technique that I taught to be rather foolproof. Follow the instructions and it works. Don't follow the instructions exactly, but practice it consistently enough, and it still works. Either way, *it works*. I also discovered that I was pretty good at teaching beginning meditators, probably because I could relate to their frustrations and speak intimately from direct experience about the pain points and inherent skepticism surrounding the ancient practice.

Now, it's my turn to teach you.

MY PROMISE

After over fifteen years as a practitioner and training thousands of students, I've become expert at teaching just about anyone how to succeed in meditation without really trying. And yes, I'm aware that the subtitle of this book is inspired by a popular musical about business, but it's also a perfect description for the very counterintuitive approach to meditation I've followed and taught, which is rooted in this time-tested principle: most people who *don't* enjoy meditation are possibly trying too hard.

In this book, my goal is to offer you the same real-world meditation principles, practical techniques, and commonsense tips that have helped me enjoy and benefit from meditation. I've taught these principles to countless beginning and veteran meditators who have used them to take their practice to more satisfying levels and, consequently, have experienced a more blissful life outside of meditation. After all, the true value of meditation is not what happens to us during meditation but how we show up in life as a result of our daily meditation practice.

My definition of success in meditation is very simple: a meditation practice that leaves you with a tangible feeling of bliss (as if you took a hot bubble bath for your mind) *and* which you look forward to doing with great anticipation (similar to how someone with a sweet tooth looks forward to eating dessert at the end of a meal, or how an exercise junkie wakes up looking forward to her workout). It's no exaggeration to say that once I train someone how to meditate, they happily make meditation a daily priority—even if they had previously convinced themselves that they didn't have time, or that their mind was too busy to meditate.

Whether you're a brand-new or experienced meditator, I want to help you move meditation out of the "I have to do" category (to which we relegate chores like housework or visits to the dentist) and into the "I *get* to do" category, which we reserve for those activities we relish and anticipate with delight (such as long naps, Sunday brunches, romantic intimacy, and vacations).

YOU'RE IN GOOD COMPANY

Because I teach primarily in Los Angeles and New York, many of my clients have been A-list Hollywood actors, professional athletes, and other boldface names in the world of entertainment and the arts. But the overwhelming majority of my clients are like you and me: ordinary people with places to go, bills to pay, and not a lot of extra time on their hands. They are college students, high-school dropouts, working parents, doctors, retirees, middle managers, baristas, firefighters, starving artists, yoga instructors, and even other meditation teachers. Regardless of background or age or fame or fortune, we all have the same basic needs: to be rested, to be adaptable to change, to be happy. And we have the same basic wants: to be more resilient to life's inevitable dramas, and to successfully adapt to the endless demands and pressures thrown our way by what can sometimes feel like a cruel and unforgiving world.

There is no amount of money or material possessions that will lead to everlasting happiness. You might be surprised to discover how many of my wealthy and famous clients seek me out because they are restless, unhappy, or reliant on pharmaceuticals to help them sleep at night or keep their anxiety at bay. Many are stressed. In that sense, stress is the great unifier: over the years, I've found that managing stress drives many more people to meditation than the proposition of increasing bliss.

Doctors call stress "the silent killer" for its relentless and stealthy ability to wreak havoc on nearly every aspect of physical and emotional health. It's also the enemy of our ability to access our full potential. But daily meditation is our Superman, because it's been shown to defeat stress more effectively than almost any other activity or intervention.

In these pages, I want to help you discover the physical rest and mental clarity that I've personally seen daily meditation provide to thousands, and in the process show you how to make meditation the consistent, non-negotiable, and deeply rewarding activity that it deserves to be. Ultimately, you will reach a point where you'll wonder how you managed to go so long without an enjoyable daily meditation practice—and the daily bliss that it brings.

HOW TO USE THIS BOOK

Admittedly, it's not easy to learn how to meditate from books. Some would say it's impossible. The main reason is that meditation, like swimming or bicycling, requires lots of practice, as opposed to just reading about it. Another reason is that meditation requires guidance, and since you'll have to close your eyes in order to practice, it's not possible to read the guidance with your eyes closed.

As a long-term practitioner of meditation, I agree wholeheartedly with these critiques. At the same time, I sincerely feel that you'll find *Bliss More* to be a rare exception. Unlike many authors of meditation books, all I've done every day for the last ten years is teach people from all walks of life how to meditate *without* the need for guidance. And prior to that, I dabbled in just about every meditation technique for many years, and studied everything I could get my hands on related to the topic. I know from experience how easy it is to fail, how slippery bliss can feel (when you're trying too hard to meditate), and what it takes to build a rock-solid daily habit.

I've studied and dissected meditation from every angle, I've been back and forth to India (the source of meditation) several times, and in the process, I've gleaned unique insights on how to show busy people with busy minds how to get the most out of a daily meditation practice. More important, I can show you how to avoid the pitfalls and obstacles that are so commonplace in the practice that they've come to be mistaken for "correct" meditation. I'm certain that, no matter who you are, my straight-talk approach will save you a lot of time and help you finally enjoy meditation. And I believe that with the right kind of instruction, catering specifically to people who have rarely or never enjoyed meditating enough to make it a daily practice, it's very possible to learn how to succeed in meditation, even from a book.

I take a unique approach in this book by *not* offering you a dozen different techniques to choose from. I feel that the last thing most readers need is more choice, which would quickly lead to analysis paralysis. Instead, based on my extensive teaching and personal experience, I'm presenting you with what I feel is the easiest and most effective approach to meditation. I even call it the E.A.S.Y. approach—this is the approach I've taught to people who, for whatever reason, couldn't make it to one of my live meditation trainings. If you're teaching yourself to meditate, the E.A.S.Y. approach is custom made for you. This is what I recommend for skeptics or anyone who is interested in meditating but unsure about their ability to sit still and calm their mind.

I also wrote this for people who were like me in the beginning: you have an existing meditation practice but don't enjoy it. Or you've concluded that you are incapable of meditating but sit down to do it anyway because your peer group is doing it, and you know on some level it's good for you. This book is explicitly *not* written for people who already enjoy their current meditation practice. But even if you're in that category, you may still discover some refinements within.

In Part One, "How to Enjoy Meditation: The Technique," I will offer you a sort of meditation primer that covers the fundamentals, such as how to sit; how to effectively and reliably settle your busy mind; and how exactly to deal with sleep, noises, and bothersome thoughts. This is the straightforward, how-to instruction part of the book (with a personal touch—I'll share my own insights along the way, including what has worked beautifully and what hasn't worked in my experience). I have presented these commonsense lessons in a way that will help you establish a daily practice quickly and with a minimum of effort but with optimum results. While I know some of you may be tempted to skip around, for best results I highly recommend reading Part One in the order presented.

You'll get the most out of Part Two, "Why We Meditate: The Benefits," once you've gotten the fundamentals down and have meditated as instructed at least a few times on your own. In Part Two I'll explore the real-world benefits of daily meditation practice, including some stories "from the field" as told by my students—people like you who were in search of a nourishing daily practice, learned an effective technique, and eventually made meditation a non-negotiable daily activity. I'll show you how to competently track your progress and verify everything I teach you through your own direct experiences. And by the end, you'll join the ranks of thousands of others who know how to succeed in meditation *without really trying*.

Though the E.A.S.Y. approach is unique to this book, it is based on timeless meditation principles that have been taught by meditation gurus, mainly in India, for thousands of years. I want to properly acknowledge their role in this process of learning. If you ever have an opportunity to study with a meditation guru, or travel to India and experience the source of meditation, I highly recommend it. It will upgrade your relationship with the practice even more, as there's no book that can properly articulate what it's like to sit at the feet of a true master or meditate along the banks of the Ganges River in northern India!

If you have never meditated before and are wondering how long you should meditate for each session, I recommend beginning with a minimum dose of ten minutes and a maximum of twenty minutes per session.

At the most, you will meditate no more than twice a day—once in the morning, and again in the afternoon or early evening. That's it—no need for more, and in fact I warn against it. Understand: this is an extremely powerful technique, and therefore it's not recommended that you practice it more than twice daily, or right before bed (you'll see why as you read further).

Also, meditation alone shouldn't be used as a treatment or cure for illness, medical problems, or mental health issues. Do not stop taking any medications or deviate from your existing healing routine without first consulting your doctor. Please use these tips responsibly and adhere to the recommended suggestions.

Learning Meditation from a Book?

Although I teach Vedic meditation, I'm *not* teaching you that style in this book because, frankly, Vedic meditation can't be taught properly from a book. Like Transcendental Meditation, Vedic meditation is a technique that can only be taught in person, because the entire learning process involves having contact with the teacher, who teaches you in person and supports you in your practice well beyond your initial training. To start Vedic meditation, you must be "initiated" into the Vedic spiritual tradition by attending a sacred *puja* ceremony, which is performed in Sanskrit by your teacher. Afterward, your teacher whispers a personalized mantra into your ear that you will use exclusively for your Vedic meditation practice; for best results, mantras should only be heard as a whisper, and never read in a book or even written down by the practitioner.

Although this is not Vedic meditation, you will find this E.A.S.Y. meditation technique and accompanying "Settling Sound" (a general-use mantra, coming up in Chapter 3) to be more than sufficient for helping you understand the inner workings of meditation and assisting you in beginning an enjoyable meditation practice, or improving upon your existing practice. You may find the knowledge presented in this book to be extremely counterintuitive—often it will be the exact opposite of the instructions you've heard for years in yoga classes, guided meditation circles, or other conventional meditation settings. So I recommend having an open mind and being willing to try everything before forming an opinion about whether it's useful or not, or as beneficial as what you've tried in the past.

Part One

HOW TO ENJOY
MEDITATION
The Technique

The E.A.S.Y. Meditation Technique

1. Sit comfortably.

2. Use an easy-to-see timing device, ideally *not* an alarm.

3. Calculate your finish time (ten to twenty minutes).

4. Close your eyes.

5. Passively think the sound "ah-hum."

6. Let yourself simultaneously get lost in your thoughts.

7. When you remember that you're meditating,
passively begin thinking "ah-hum" again.

8. Peek freely and often at the time.

9. Once you're done, wait a minute or two before opening your eyes.

10. Come out slowly.

Recommended Schedule

• Meditate *once in the morning,* upon awakening, for ten to twenty
minutes. Sit up and make sure you have comfortable back support.

• Meditate again *once in the afternoon or early evening* for ten to
twenty minutes. Do not exceed two meditations per day.

1

GET COMFORTABLE

For years, I've lived about a ten-minute stroll from Venice beach, a hotbed for activities such as yoga, meditation, and surfing. Unlike the first two practices, surfing has utterly eluded me.

I'm embarrassed to admit that I've only been surfing a few times. Surfing has made frequent appearances on my New Year's resolution lists over the past decade—but I just haven't been a fan of activities that involve swimming in freezing-cold, murky (not to mention sharky) waters. Plus, to me it doesn't seem like an easy sport for most beginners—I would need to seek the guidance of someone with the patience of Job to show me the ropes.

However warped my ideas about surfing are, it is a revered activity in this part of the world, practically a religion. If I were to walk around my neighborhood complaining about how "surfing sucks" (mainly because I'm not that good at it), I would certainly make some enemies pretty quickly. The number of people I know who simply *love* surfing are too many to count—several even consider surfing to be their daily meditation—and they never stop trying to coerce me to join them one morning in their saltwater sanctuary. But I still haven't invested the time and energy to learn how to do it properly, so for me, surfing isn't fun.

Deep down, I know I'm being stubborn and ignorant. But I also respect the fact that there's more to surfing than giving it a handful of halfhearted tries. I don't assume that surfing is mainly about showing up at a beach with a wet suit and a surfboard. Any experienced surfer will tell you that there's a lot more to it than that. For starters, don't you also need to know how long a board to use, depending on your height and experience level? And how thick a wet suit to wear in relation to the water temperature? And how to carry the board into the water so a wave doesn't cause it to flip up and crack your head open? And how to hop on the board properly and paddle out beyond the break without wearing yourself out before you even get started? And how to turn properly? Where to sit on the board so you're prepared to catch a wave? How to pop up? And, most important, what to do if you have to pee in the middle of a set? (Spoiler alert: you go in your suit. Maybe that's the real reason I haven't started surfing.)

The point is, if you don't know all of these little details and finer points, surfing is going to be a very miserable experience indeed, and, like me, you'll probably never enjoy it enough to make it a daily ritual.

Many people have had a similar experience with meditation, because (as I did in my first few years) they figured at the outset that meditating is about sitting on a cushion, closing your eyes, and paying attention to your breathing. Voilà—you look the part, so now you're meditating. In other words, they started meditating without properly understanding the ins and outs of the practice. How to position your body for best results? How long to sit for? How long is too short? How long is too long? How to handle your busy mind? What to do if you fall asleep? What if the dog jumps up on your lap or the doorbell rings? What happens if you have to pee in the middle of meditation? (Don't worry, it's not like surfing.) What does it mean if you start crying in meditation, or if you begin feeling depressed, or if your body heats up? What's the most effective way to time your meditations? How do you track progress? How do you know when you're trying too hard? How do you inspire others to join you in meditation without causing them to run in the opposite direction?

If you don't know the answers to these questions, even a basic meditation practice is going to feel pretty miserable and, like me with surfing (and with my initial experiences with meditation), you will ignorantly conclude that you are incapable of meditating with success. But all it really means is that no one has shown you the inner workings of meditation—until now. As you'll see, with a combination of knowledge and practice, you will become like my surfing enthusiast friends: waking up at the crack of dawn excited to sit for your meditation not just because it's good for you but because you'll finally know what you're doing, and that makes the experience *so* much more beneficial, enjoyable, and fun. And my prediction is you'll want all of your friends to join you as well.

They say misery loves company. Well, bliss does, too! And the more blissful you feel from the inside out, the more you'll want to share with others the daily practice that is the source of your inner happiness. Best of all, you no longer have to make other non-meditation activities your substitute for meditation. For you, *meditation* will be your meditation.

You can think of the fundamentals we're about to explore as being a bit like the lessons you would receive at surfing school. The one or two times I took surfing lessons, they first had us practice paddling and popping up on the board while lying in the sand. Only after we mastered the sand exercises did we set foot in the water. In the same way, you've first got to understand the mechanical underpinnings of meditation. So let's dive right in. Sitting comfortably is the first step in the E.A.S.Y. approach.

IT'S NOT ABOUT THE OMMMMMM

One day my little niece inquired about meditation and what it means to teach people to meditate. As I began explaining the process to her in greater detail than her seven-year-old's interest level merited, she cut me off by announcing that she would have no need for my services, because she already knew how to meditate.

Amused by her confidence, I asked her to demonstrate how meditation works. She then crossed her legs, sat up straight, poked out her little chest, drew her shoulders back, placed the back of her hands on top of her knees with her fingers in an upside-down "okay" configuration, and began loudly chanting, "Ommmm, ommmm, ommmm," interspersed with fits of giggles.

Actually, she wasn't too far off from what many Westerners feel is the "ideal" posture for meditating. As the thinking goes, if we want to be like Buddha, we must sit like Buddha to meditate, while chanting or focusing on a foreign sound—with no moving, no scratching, no succumbing to discomfort or pain.

Where do we get this stiff, rigid caricature of a meditator? The answer is that for a long time Westerners have associated the practice of meditation too literally with Eastern monasticism—meaning we view meditation mainly as a monastic practice that works better the more austere we can be.

The stereotype of the soft-spoken, mild-mannered meditator who observes celibacy, vegetarianism, and detachment from the material world is linked to two distinct populations from history—the Indian *bramacharya* (monk) and the *sannyasa* (renunciate). Monks and renunciates have been regarded throughout history as the supreme authorities on meditation because they have willingly sacrificed material pursuits and endured great physical hardship in order to prioritize meditation and other spiritual practices, with the ultimate goal of achieving spiritual liberation. So naturally, we Westerners assume that if we too want to become spiritually liberated through meditation or other means, we must look and act the part of the monk or renunciate—not realizing that there's another population of people who have also enjoyed the practice of meditation in tandem with the monks and renunciates throughout history, but without sacrificing their worldly lifestyle. This person is known as the *grihastha*, or householder.

The Rise of the Householder

In Indian culture, you and I would be considered householders—that is, if like me, you are also interested in relationships, jobs, hobbies, having good credit, eating a variety of foods, having intimacy, and hanging with friends. Householder isn't a bad word or an insult, either. In fact, the monks see householders as crucial members of society because we are the ones who produce the food and wealth that helps to sustain everyone else, including all of the monks and renunciates. Plus we are needed to produce more potential monks in the form of offspring.

Monks, by definition, don't have a strong desire to engage in material or worldly pursuits, and would rather spend most or all of their time working to achieve spiritual liberation. Householders are naturally more engaged in the material world in every way (romantically, professionally, and socially). To a householder, the thought of making monk-like sacrifices in order to gain spiritual liberation seems like a big ask, and therefore carries little weight in our hearts and minds. It's not our inclination to make such sacrifices when we may have careers that we are passionate about, families to care for, and other worldly pursuits that excite us equally.

In order to join a monastic order, you may be asked to first give up many "impure" householder behaviors, such as eating meat, drinking wine, smoking, and sex. These behaviors are seen as potentially distracting or destructive to the monk's spiritual studies and ultimate goal of liberation. But the approach to meditation for a householder doesn't require such extreme external changes in order to begin.

That said, once you commit yourself to a regular meditation practice, you may experience internal shifts that will positively influence external changes in your behavior. For instance, I've had meditation students who naturally lost the desire to smoke and drink as their meditation practice got stronger. I've seen others who have become more mindful about who they spend their time with, both socially and intimately. In the householder approach, the benefits accrue more organically, and are not seen as required lifestyle changes that prohibit you from starting. This is great news because it means you don't have to be a perfect human to begin meditating. The other piece of good news? You don't have to sit like a monk to be a meditator!

No Monk Experience Necessary

If you've ever thought that any of the following were impediments to enjoying a successful meditation practice, you've fallen for the I-need-to-be-a-monk-in-order-to-start-meditating stereotype:

- Being a smoker
- Being a meat eater
- Having young children or pets
- Living in a noisy environment
- Having a demanding spouse
- Having a demanding job
- Being strapped for time
- Being unable to sit still for very long
- Being unable to keep your eyes closed
- Being unable to cross your legs
- Being unable to sit with your back straight
- Having an extremely busy mind

THE ART OF SITTING

Before I had the incredibly good fortune of meeting my meditation teacher after years of struggling, my idea of meditation was no different from how I described my niece's at the beginning of this chapter—except I also had notoriously tight hamstrings, which prohibited me from being able to sit with my legs crossed and back straight for more than a few minutes without writhing in pain. That was a big reason why I initially dreaded the idea of meditating whenever my friend Will would suggest it.

And that's also why I welcomed with delight the first instruction I received from my meditation teacher, which was to sit comfortably with my back supported. Get off the floor and sit on the couch, MV suggested, or in a chair if you prefer. But be comfortable. "Seriously?" I wondered. "But is that *real* meditation?"

He reminded me that meditation was never meant to be something that others watched you do, and instead of being concerned about what it looks like on the outside while meditating, I should be more concerned about what my body feels like on the inside.

Finally, after all those years, I had permission to sit comfortably! And the difference it made in the quality of my experiences was like a godsend.

If you've ever read Elizabeth Gilbert's popular memoir *Eat Pray Love,* you may remember she described her experiences with meditating in that dank Indian ashram for three months as very difficult, mostly due to her body position. She apparently sat for hours upon hours in discomfort while attempting to reach the elusive *turīya* state, which is the moment in meditation when you become unaware of time and space and, therefore, genuinely unbothered by surface noises, thoughts, insects buzzing around, or sensations. Instead, you are experiencing pure inner bliss. She eventually got there near the end of her three months, but only briefly. And it sounded like it was an uphill battle.

I'm not suggesting that the classic monastic meditation position of crossed legs and straight back was incorrect for Elizabeth, or for anyone else who meditates. Rather, it's just a tad extreme for all people who spend a lot of time sitting at desks and in cars each day.

To put the two different approaches into context, imagine that you want to start jogging for exercise. If you're new to jogging and not athletically inclined, your beginner-jogging regimen will be understandably modest. In other words, you don't need to adopt the training and diet program of a world-class track-and-field athlete in order to jog around the park after work. Doing so would be considered unnecessarily extreme, especially if you have a full-time job, a family, and hobbies. But if you desired to compete in the Olympics, then modeling your training program after a champion's regimen makes complete sense, because your goals and priorities would obviously be vastly different from the casual jogger's.

Similarly, monks are like the Olympic athletes of meditation. That's why they tend to adhere to a stricter diet and practice regimen. But we have to remember that monks aren't facing the same daily demands as the average householder who works nine to five, and may have additional family and recreational activities to prioritize.

In short, what the householder requires from meditation is vastly different from what the monk desires—and the number one requirement for you in the case of meditation is comfort when it comes to your sitting position.

SIT LIKE YOU'RE BINGE-WATCHING TV

Among the thousands of people I've trained to meditate, I've found yoga teachers the most challenging, because by and large, yoga teachers promote the classic seated posture known as "lotus pose" as the gold standard for sitting in meditation. If you're not familiar, to sit in lotus pose, you must cross your legs so deeply that the soles of your feet face the sky. This is considered by yogis to be the optimal position for meditating. And if lotus is not possible, then the next best option is to sit on a meditation cushion or a yoga bolster with your legs crossed until you are flexible enough to work up to lotus.

I once had a yoga teacher arrive at my studio carrying a yoga bolster, even though I told him in the orientation that we would be sitting comfortably to meditate. When it was time for us to meditate, he instinctively reached for his bolster and positioned it beneath his hips so he could sit as tall as possible in the classical monastic meditation position. Long spine. Chin lifted. Legs crossed. And palms up.

The problem was I had just spent an hour reiterating the importance of sitting comfortably in meditation, and how doing so would free his mind to drop more easily into a settled state. He did not look as comfortable on the bolster as he had when he had been sitting on my couch (when we were doing all that talking). When I asked how he felt in his cross-legged position, he explained that the bolster helped align his hip flexors.

I tried another tack: "Where do you sit when you're binge-watching your favorite television show?"

"On my couch or in bed," he replied.

"Could you show me how you sit?" I asked. He got up off the bolster and sat back on the couch to demonstrate his TV-watching posture. His feet were up on the ottoman as he settled into the back cushion.

"Great," I said. "You watch hours of television in that position, so it's comfortable, no? That's how I recommend you sit for meditation!" He remained skeptical but gave my suggestion a try, and reported afterward that the meditation was significantly more relaxing than any he had ever experienced in yoga class. I responded, "I know the feeling."

How to Sit Comfortably

Sitting comfortably means you ideally want to stay off the ground and sit on your sofa, or in a reading chair, or anywhere else that feels effortless for you. It also means that you want your back supported. You should still sit relatively upright, but your back does not have to be straight, and your shoulders don't have to be drawn back. Likewise, your hands and feet can be at ease, and you could even stretch your legs out in front of you if you find that more comfortable. You can use pillows to provide extra comfort to your lower back, or cross your arms while you meditate. And you may wrap your shoulders or legs, or your whole body in a blanket or shawl. Again, we're going for supreme comfort and coziness here.

Avoid "Position Shaming"

Sitting with your back as straight as a board can get in the way of successful (effortless and enjoyable) meditation, and thinking that you're not meditating *correctly* if you're not sitting up completely erect is a form of what I call "position shaming." If I had to write a dictionary definition for position shaming it would be this: *The practice of making yourself or another meditator feel bad for not sitting up completely straight in meditation; meditating in a way that looks good for the camera but feels physically strenuous and uncomfortable.*

If I asked you to choose which of the images below is the more "correct" meditation posture, my guess (based on asking lots of people this very question) is that you'd choose position A, with the straight back, and say that position B looks "too relaxed."

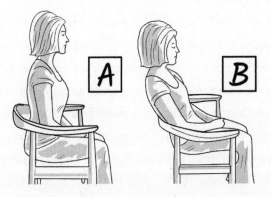

But as a householder looking to enjoy meditation, you may find that position A actually works against you, while position B is more conducive to having a deeper, more enjoyable experience.

There's actually a simple biological reason why the straight-back meditation position on the left (A) has made many millions of meditations throughout history feel laborious. It's because sitting so straight requires us to exert physical activity in order to hold the body in position. And unnatural physical activity *of any kind* leads to an *increase* in mental activity, not the decrease in mental activity that both novice and experienced meditators desire. In order to have a more satisfying meditation experience, it's highly recommended to sit in a way that reduces unnecessary physical activity. In other words, it's not that you *should* sit comfortably when meditating. It's that you *need* to sit comfortably to meditate with success.

Inevitably, some of my students resist this advice or are even offended by it because their previous yoga or meditation instructor has position-shamed them into thinking that sitting up straight is the only way to open their chakras and cultivate proper meditative energy. But at this point in your meditation practice, when you're simply trying to enjoy it long enough for it to become a daily habit, I urge you not to be overly concerned with chakras or energy flow, or even with hip alignment. For you, right now, *comfort* is the main priority. When your body is comfortable, the desired mental experience will follow quite effortlessly, especially once you learn how to exploit the nature of the mind for your benefit (Chapter 2 will help you with this). For now, study and adopt the examples of ideal meditation body positions presented below.

Ideal seated positions:

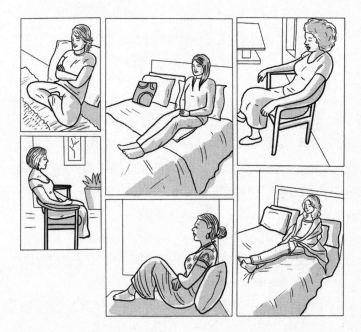

Put It to the Test: Find Your Sitting Position

How do you feel right now, as you're reading this page? Are you sitting comfortably? Give proper sitting a shot before we move on. Go to your bed, sit on a couch, or find a comfortable chair. Just get cozy, with your back supported in any way that works for you. When you're positioned comfortably, close your eyes, and have at it for about ten minutes if you can. Don't worry about your breathing or where your mind is going—this exercise is just about finding a comfortable seat. If you fall asleep easily, that's okay, too—there's a good reason for that, which we'll go over later.

WHERE SHOULD YOU MEDITATE? HINT: *NOT* ON THE BEACH

Now that you know the optimum way to sit for an enjoyable meditation, you may be wondering about *where* to sit. I'm not talking about which chair to choose. I'm talking about the overall environment for enjoying meditation—a place that's conducive to achieving a settled mind. If we take our cues from the Internet, it's easy to conclude that the best places to meditate are:

- An all-white, sparsely furnished, sun-drenched room, perhaps in front of a meditation altar
- Outside in nature, perhaps on a cliffside, overlooking a beautiful vista
- On the beach at sunset
- In the middle of a field of grass under a blue sky
- On a rock, or while perched under a bodhi tree
- Next to the lotus pond in a Japanese Zen garden

It's easy to further conclude that even if you were to find one of the aforementioned "ideal" meditation environments, you would be incapable of meditating properly without mala beads, a meditation cushion, a yoga mat, a blanket, or comfortable yoga pants—oh, and don't forget your tealight candles, incense, wind chimes, and Zen stones.

Of course, most of these ideas come from stock photographs that are about as true to real-life meditation as your social media "friends" are to your real friends. In other words, they represent a fantasy. Real people living busy lives don't meditate in those kinds of environments. Real people can meditate successfully on their ten-year-old couch, in bed alone or next to their snoring partner, in their comfortable reading chair, in the passenger seat of their car, at work, at the kitchen table, in church, on a bean bag, in the backseat during a road trip, on a park bench, or in a bus or plane seat.

And that's as it should be, because if you are waiting to find yourself atop a cliffside or in a white, sparsely furnished room in order to feel like you can meditate, you're only going to meditate sporadically, and you're going to mistakenly conclude that what little benefit you are able to derive from your practice is magically linked to your serene environment—which couldn't be further from the truth. Basically, *anywhere* where you can sit comfortably with your back supported is the ideal place to meditate.

If you're wondering about the noise factor: while it's preferable to have a quiet environment, thinking that you need perfect quiet in order to meditate properly is a common amateur mistake, too. But now that you're reading this book, you are going to quickly evolve beyond amateur status and become a meditation pro. Meditation pros don't require perfectly quiet or serene environments in which to meditate. Instead, they know from experience that meditation *creates* the quiet inside. Moving forward, we want to graduate from the idea that we need a controlled environment to meditate. This way, meditation becomes portable, and mobility leads to consistency.

You've learned about the importance of maintaining a comfortable body position while meditating and are letting go of any old notions you had about the "perfect" environment. Now, starting in Chapter 2, you're ready to explore the nature of the meditating mind, the anatomy of thinking, and the ideal internal cues that lead to success in meditation. And as soon as you begin to enjoy it, you will be successful.

2

ALL THOUGHTS MATTER

Before we get into the nuts and bolts of the meditating mind, I first invite you to try a little thought experiment. It's simple and only takes thirty seconds. In a moment, I want you to close your eyes and focus all of your attention on one image: polar bears. I know, random. But give it a try, and do not think about anything else *other* than polar bears if you can help it. After you guesstimate that about thirty seconds is up, you may open your eyes and continue on to the next page. But take half a minute to do this exercise right now! Seriously. Don't continue reading until you do it.

Did you do it? If so, did your mind sound something like this:

"Okay, think only of polar bears . . . ?"

"White polar bears . . ."

"This is kind of silly. I can't believe I'm doing it . . ."

"I'm feeling a bit antsy."

"Why is he having us do this anyway?"

"White bears . . ."

"I wonder how much time has passed . . ."

"I've got to get dinner started . . ."

"Oh boy, I did it again—I knew my mind wouldn't let me focus."

Most people, upon experiencing the above scattering of un-related thoughts along with a sprinkling of polar bear thoughts, would assume that their brain is being mischievous, or that they lack the ability to focus—particularly when it comes to meditation. But before you draw any conclusions about what that could mean, let's try one more quick experiment.

This time, I'd like for you to close your eyes and do the opposite—for thirty seconds, allow your mind to roam free but avoid polar bear thoughts. In other words, you can think any thought you want, *as long as it's not about polar bears.* Close your eyes . . . and remember, no thoughts about polar bears, okay? Go!

I'll bet this was your experience:

"White bears"

"Uh oh . . ."

"More white bears!"

"It happened again!"

"Polar bears."

"Polar bears."

"Not more polar bears!"

"They're everywhere!"

"I can't stop thinking about white bears."

"Am I in a polar bear movie?"

"I need to make dinner . . . for polar bears."

"Crap, I knew my mind wouldn't let me un-focus . . ."

Be honest—were you unsuccessful in *not* thinking about polar bears just then? If so, guess what? Whether you experienced a scattering of random thoughts while trying to focus on polar bears or a barrage of polar bear thoughts while trying to block them out, it means your brain is completely normal.

THE POLAR BEAR EFFECT

I am not the first to ask people to think—or not think—about polar bears. In 1863, Russian author Fyodor Dostoevsky wrote the following in his travel journal: *"Try to pose for yourself this task: not to think of a polar bear, and you will see that the cursed thing will come to mind every minute."*

Inspired by Dostoevsky's amateur experiments with thought suppression, a Harvard social psychologist named Dr. Daniel

Wegner orchestrated a proper study in the 1980s to find out whether it's possible for someone to control her mind by trying *not* to think about specific subjects—in this case, polar bears.

To test the theory, individuals were brought into a room and given a bell like one you might see in a hotel lobby. They were instructed to think about polar bears for five minutes, and to ring the bell each time they had a deliberate polar bear thought. Then they were asked to purposely allow their minds to wander to any thought they wished with the exception of polar bears for five minutes. If they accidentally thought about the polar bears, they were told to ring the bell.

The result? Lots more ringing when subjects *weren't* supposed to think about polar bears. The conclusion: no matter how smart or calm you are, if you try to focus on a particular thought, you *will* get distracted. And if you attempt to ban a thought, you will be able to think of nothing else.

Below is an illustration of how we experience our minds while engaged in focused thinking (such as during the polar bear experiment). I've segmented the mind into three zones: the

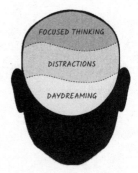

focused-thinking zone, the distraction zone, and the daydreaming zone.

Thought suppressing means we want to stay in the focused-thinking zone and keep the distractions and daydreaming at bay. But as Dr. Wegner's study showed—and as you yourself likely experienced when I asked you to think and then not think of polar bears—whether we try to focus on something specific or not, we inevitably experience a significant amount of distraction. Even if you were able to keep yourself focused on (or off) polar bears for thirty seconds, try doing it for one or two minutes and notice how you experience a fair amount of distracting thoughts. I'm defining distracting thoughts as any type of thoughts that are unrelated to the act of focusing on the task at hand. Instead, we may have thoughts about the noise quality of our environment, guesses about the underlying intention of the exercise, or thoughts about our immediate past or about what we're going to do after we're done reading, sensations in or around our body, or any other thoughts outside of the point of focus.

The illustration below is more likely what you experienced while you were trying to think of polar bears:

The random scattering of unrelated thoughts that you experienced while trying to focus was a symptom of your mind dipping into the distraction zone.

Now, here's your mind while trying *not* to think of polar bears:

When given permission to think about *anything* except for polar bear thoughts, the polar bear thoughts move into the distraction zone. Interestingly, Dr. Wegner and his team found that there actually is a part of the brain that can suppress thoughts, but at the same time, another part of the brain will keep checking like an overbearing mother to make sure that the thought is still being suppressed, which adds to the feeling of obsessing about that particular thought—in this case, polar bears!

Either way, the diagrams are virtually the same. The only difference is in which content is considered to be distracting—the unrelated thoughts in the first experience and the polar bear thoughts in the second.

This mental quandary can appear problematic, particularly when we consider how we will navigate a fifteen- or twenty-

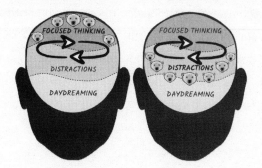

minute meditation without having to go to battle with our "busy" mind.

But here's an important point: so-called distractions are a part of the thinking process and aren't a bad or less-than thing. So don't categorize them that way. Once you realize and accept this point, you'll have less frustration in meditation.

EXPOSING THE "BUSY MIND" MYTH

You would not be unique if you've caught yourself being consumed by random thoughts while meditating. You would also not be alone in interpreting them as distractions and attempting to refocus even harder on the task at hand: staying focused. But maintaining strict focus usually involves creating a sense of separation between you and your thoughts. Someone may have even instructed you to think "I am not my thoughts, I am not my thoughts, I am not my thoughts," over and over during meditation.

But do you see the problem with this instruction? You're

being asked to use your thoughts to convince yourself that you are *not* your thoughts. If you find this confusing, join the club, because this is what I also found initially confusing when I was dabbling in meditation and trying to understand the mechanics. How do you stop thoughts while using thoughts to not think the thoughts you want to stop thinking? "Don't think!" is a thought, as is "Why am I still thinking?"

This mental house of mirrors can quickly devolve into you blaming yourself for your inability to stop your intrusive thoughts, erroneously concluding that you are burdened with a "monkey mind," which is the classic description of a mind that acts like a drunken monkey that is swinging erratically in a tree after having been stung by a bee!

Considering that humans reportedly experience between sixty thousand and ninety thousand individual thoughts per day, the feeling of a monkey mind isn't that uncommon. If we're measuring busyness by the sheer *quantity* of thoughts (an average of three thoughts per second, according to some speculations), everyone technically has a busy mind. This means, no matter how busy you feel your mind is, as far as quantity is concerned, it's technically no more or less like the drunken monkey than my mind, or anyone else's.

Why might our minds feel uniquely busy? It's been suggested that of the tens of thousands of thoughts we supposedly have each day, as many as 90 percent of them are recycled from yesterday. Assuming that's true, then our monkey mind is more or less swinging toward the same recycled thoughts, and processing the same recycled information, with the same frequency, in the same way, day after day after day after day. In other words, without some sort of intervention like meditation, the way you felt about your life yesterday is probably how you're going to feel about it today, tomorrow, and the next day. The way you handled a work problem last week is probably the same way you're going to at least initially think about handling a similar problem if it happens again this week. And with each passing day, those thoughts become more hardwired, ensuring that they'll come up again tomorrow.

This may seem rigid and unnatural, but that's how humans have evolved to adapt to their environment. If we had to wake up each day with a blank mental slate and relearn that we should look both ways before crossing the street, or not play with fire, we might not survive long enough to reproduce. We can thank our brain chemistry for this conditioning. It reminds our body

"We found this in your brain."

of what we've already learned, and makes sure repeated experiences become more hardwired each day. This is the nature of habit building. All habits—good and bad—are part mental, and part chemical.

Case in point, I wrote a good amount of this book in one of my favorite neighborhood cafés, because they have comfortable seats and offer unlimited refills of green iced tea, which used to be my preferred beverage to sip on while writing. After several months of coming in and ordering my iced tea, the baristas began greeting me by guessing my order, "Iced tea?" I'd nod, and a minute later the cold beverage would appear on the counter. Eventually they stopped asking and just started making it automatically as soon as they saw me enter the café. By that point, my preference was actually swinging toward hot tea. However, I felt obligated to take the iced tea only because they kept automatically making it for me on sight. To this day, I haven't had the heart to tell them that I don't always want the iced tea.

In this analogy, our busy mind is like the barista trying to anticipate what we need or want, and trying to cut down on the unnecessary steps to get us there. It's not trying to punish us or make us feel stuck by harboring certain negative thoughts. It's just being efficient by adapting to the past—"If this is the way you've handled that aspect of your life over the last three months or three years, or thirty years, what makes today any different?" And this cycle of efficiency is what creates what I call the Groundhog Day Effect, named after the 1993 movie where Bill Murray's character was caught in a weird time loop and had to keep reliving the same one day in his life (which happened to be Groundhog Day) until he could figure out how to change his life to change his fate. Our repetitive thoughts can make us feel as though we're trapped in a similar kind of nightmare.

This is one of the reasons the beneficial results of personal development courses, diet plans, and exercise routines often don't last as long as we hope without effectively rewiring the root cause of a potential relapse—our brain. Otherwise, we may start down a new path, fired up with enthusiasm about all of the wonderful changes we are going to make in our lives because we intellectually understand the errors of our old ways and all of our blind spots and contradictory beliefs have been sufficiently exposed. But our new worldview can't outmaneuver the neural wiring that has solidified in our brains after literally years in the making. And a month or two later, we're back standing in our own way again, frustrated because we can't liberate ourselves from habits that are obviously counterproductive and unsustainable—even though we know better. Alas, losing weight, finding love, or getting out of debt will have to wait. Or worse, we conclude that there's something wrong with us. But the reality is it's just biology.

Yet, failed attempts to instantly calm our minds in meditation can quickly snuff out our optimism about our ability to meditate and find bliss, especially if we don't know how to properly interpret our experiences as we engage in the practice. *Am I supposed to feel scattered in meditation? Where are the calm thoughts? What's for dinner? Oh no!*

Unfortunately, the conventional solutions for managing this crazy-making loop leave the meditator in a situation where she feels as though the metaphorical straitjacket keeps getting tightened by the Nurse Ratched–mind (that's a *One Flew over the Cuckoo's Nest* reference—see the movie if you haven't already).

But there's an easy solution for escaping the Groundhog Day Effect and simultaneously quieting the monkey mind, and it's been hiding in plain sight this entire time.

LETTING GO OF THE TRADITIONAL APPROACH

A well-meaning meditation guide may advise you (in that stereotypically soft-spoken voice) that the best way to handle your disobedient and distracted mind is to simply "witness your thoughts, like clouds passing in the sky."

Another meditation teacher may instruct you to "dissociate from your thoughts," explaining how meditation is all about non-attachment, because your thoughts aren't *you*. Rather, they are a symptom of a mind that can't be tamed, and they should be either ignored or brushed off as irrelevant to the process.

A third meditation expert may instruct you to "let go" of the distracting thoughts you don't like in favor of the thoughts you find more beneficial or more relaxing, such as picturing yourself immersed in a ball of white light, or bathing in a waterfall.

The problem with these approaches is they all employ some degree of mental focus. Being told to "witness," "let go of," or "ignore" your thoughts is a directive that requires the additional work of exclusivity. In other words, you have to attempt to mentally exclude (block out or ban) certain perceived negative or irrelevant thoughts or sensations in favor of more positive experiences. This requires you to engage in mental activity *before engaging in the activity*.

Think about it. To let go of the unwanted thoughts, you must remind yourself continually, "Witness this thought. It is just a cloud passing," "Oops, there it is again—just let it pass," "Let go of this negative thought, and begin to think of something more positive," or "I'm just going to ignore this thought, and keep ignoring it until it goes away." Exhausting, no? That's because being task-oriented in meditation is the same as being focused. You may be watching a thought like a cloud, but you are still employing some degree of mental activity (focus), which will keep your mind feeling defeated when it experiences the inevitable distractions. Need we remember the polar bear experiment?

What you desire and how you behave in meditation are often complete opposites. You may desire a quieter, more settled mind, yet you are unknowingly taught by some meditation facilitators to actively engage in a focused activity in a great effort to quiet the mind. This doesn't make sense. How can you have a focused mind *and* a quiet mind at the same time? You can't. And this is the main problem with many conventional approaches to meditation. Basically, anytime you see or hear the word "focus" in the instruction, get ready to roll your sleeves up and go to work, because that's exactly what the experience is going to feel like— hard (and too often joyless) work.

No matter how you approach it, a blissful mind is not easy to accomplish through *increased* work in meditation. This fact is completely bewildering to many long-term practitioners because the word "focus" has been associated with correct meditation since the beginning. Yet if those same meditators are being honest, can they say that focused-attention meditation techniques have ever felt easy or enjoyable in the beginning?

Instead of boosting mental activity in an effort to settle or quiet the mind in meditation, we're going to explore what I've found to be a much easier way to achieve the desired result—first by taking a peek under the hood of the meditating mind in order to understand what it is that we're erroneously referring to as distracting thoughts, and then by accepting the one experience 99 percent of new meditators resist at the beginning of their practice.

A Better Way: Reframing the Busy Mind

If you were to stop ten strangers on the street and conduct an impromptu poll about whether they feel that they would be good at meditation, you will likely find that the overwhelming majority of the people express some doubt regarding their ability to meditate with success. If you ask why, they'll give you some variation of "my mind is *too* busy." Even people who drag themselves out of bed and force themselves to meditate each morning claim to have a busy mind. In all of my years of teaching, and conducting that impromptu poll, I've never once had someone answer, "Oh yes, I can absolutely meditate with success, no problem! My mind is always quiet and calm . . . perfect for meditation!"

Now let's change the question. Suppose you asked those same people if it's possible to be too out of shape to exercise. They would laugh at you and say, "What are you talking about? Exercise is good for people who are out of shape." Well, what if the same is true for meditation? What if concluding that your mind is too busy to meditate was as absurd as suggesting that you're too out of shape to exercise? Having an exceptional ability to focus your mind into stillness is not and never has been a prerequisite to succeeding at meditation.

Rather, think of meditation as the treadmill for the out-of-shape mind. It's the tool, not the goal, and should be treated as such. It doesn't care who you are, where you're from, or what your beliefs are. If you use it appropriately, it works. If you misuse it, it won't work. In the same way that a treadmill is useful for building up cardiovascular strength, meditation is useful for refining perceptual acuity (being able to read a room), improving mental dexterity and clarity (making fast-paced decisions in high-pressure environments), organizing thoughts, and increasing bliss (acting, speaking, and thinking from a place of inner calmness).

No matter the task, the physically in-shape version of you will always outperform the sedentary version of you. Likewise, the version of you that meditates daily will out-rest, out-think, out-intuit, out-respond, and out-perform the non-meditating version of you, every day of the week and twice on Sunday. While there are reams of scientific studies that back up this statement, I feel that it's also self-evident. And you probably feel the same way, since you're reading this book. You already agree that meditation would be good for you. In fact, I don't recall ever meeting a person who didn't feel at some level that his life would improve with a daily meditation habit. The debate has never been whether meditation was beneficial for some people and not others. The consensus is that meditation is a good thing for *any* person to incorporate into their life. In Los Angeles, meditation classes have even extended to include canines. The jury has deliberated, and the resounding verdict is yes, meditation will improve every aspect of your life (perhaps even if you have four legs and can bark).

The questions I often get from students are "Can I be good at meditation?" and "Why does something that is supposedly so good for me feel so hard to do?" This brings us back to the premise of this book, which is that meditation *needs* to feel enjoyable in order for us to stay engaged with it for long enough to get past the initial honeymoon phase and into the stabilization of happiness, where nearly every meditation feels blissful. These are common phases that long-term meditators experience. As far as daily activities stack up, meditation needs to meander its way from the "I need to" or "I should" categories into the "I get to" category. This is the only way you will keep meditation around long enough to experience the long-term benefits that a meditation practice can provide.

No matter what purpose we want to use meditation for, it *must* feel good in order for us to feel inspired enough to sit on a regular enough basis to realize those benefits, which means we have to understand the pitfalls and be ready for them. And one of the most glaring misconceptions about the tool called meditation is that it primarily involves the need to focus our way through an experience that is bound to, at some level, feel tedious or boring.

But the boring feeling can be a symptom of improperly using the tool. The secret to using the tool in the most efficient way to effortlessly access the pinnacle experience in meditation (pure bliss) is to *stop resisting the thoughts we would normally consider to be distracting, and begin leaning into our busy-mind experiences.* In other words, our success hinges on the extent to which we embrace the thinking mind itself.

MEDITATION FOR BUSY PEOPLE WITH BUSY MINDS

The key to succeeding in meditation is to treat *all* thoughts as a legitimate part of the meditating experience, regardless of the content. Say it with me: *All thoughts matter.* This is not hyperbole. The more we celebrate our thinking mind, the more transcendent and blissful our experiences will be in meditation and consequently, the richer and more spacious our experiences will become *outside* of meditation.

- The first step in celebrating the mind is to get rid of the word "distracting" when describing our unrelated thoughts in meditation.
- The next step is to liberate ourselves from the need to witness, let go of, or replace those previously unrelated thoughts with more focused or wholesome thoughts.
- Third, we should absolve ourselves from the need to

focus on any thoughts in particular or actively ignore them.

Instead of practicing exclusivity, we're going to begin practicing the opposite—treating all thoughts, sensations, emotions, desires, feelings, inspirations, or anything else we may be thinking about while meditating as 100 percent legitimate. To appreciate this novel approach, it helps to see the bigger picture of how the previously labeled distracting thoughts play a useful role in our meditation process.

In the next illustration, I've replaced the previously labeled "distraction" zone with what I'm now referring to as the "random thinking" zone. This is a deliberate word choice and an effort to help you stop seeing random thoughts in meditation as distractions (obstacles) and start seeing them simply as any thoughts that are unrelated to the knowledge (awareness) that you're meditating. In addition to that, you'll see three new zones below random thinking. The "daydreaming" zone has been re-

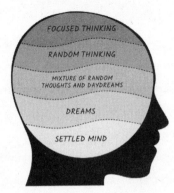

FOCUSED THINKING

RANDOM THINKING

MIXTURE OF RANDOM
THOUGHTS AND DAYDREAMS

DREAMS

SETTLED MIND

placed by "mixture of random thoughts and daydreams" and then "dreams." At the very bottom is the "settled mind" zone. These five zones encapsulate all the mental experiences that you might have within a given meditation.

Focused thinking is thinking exclusively about the task at hand, which in the case of meditation may be thoughts related to the act of meditating:

"I'm sitting on my couch meditating . . ."

"My mind is very busy while I'm meditating . . ."

"This meditation feels long . . ."

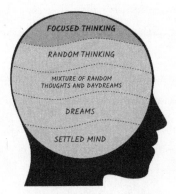

Random thinking includes thoughts that are relevant to your life, but they are otherwise unrelated to the act of meditating:

"I want to have macaroni for dinner . . ."

"I forgot to call the dentist to make an appointment . . ."

"Why hasn't my friend messaged me back . . . ?"

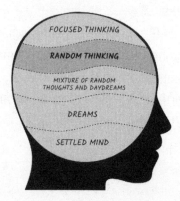

Next we have **a mixture of random thoughts and day-dreams**. Daydreams are thoughts that may make partial sense but are experienced as even more random and fragmented than normal unrelated thoughts, such as:

"I should go back to college to become a circus clown . . ."

"Maybe I'll be a clown who entertains elephants . . ."

"But only if the elephants are from Cleveland . . ."

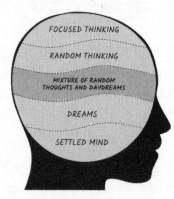

Then we have thoughts that are interpretations of **dreams**. In other words, these are thoughts that either don't make any sense or are predominantly related to sensations, emotions, or feelings, such as colored lights; feelings of floating, heaviness, or numbness (loss of feeling); or spontaneous fits of laughing, sadness, guilt, shock, or tiredness:

"That shade of blue is beautiful . . ."

"I can't feel my hands . . ."

"I'm getting sleepy . . ."

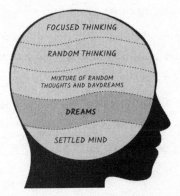

And finally, we have the **settled mind**, where pure bliss is directly experienced—pure bliss being another name for the experience of *samadhi* (union with the divine) or *nirvana* (supreme inner peace and serenity).

To the novice, this sounds like an impossibly mercurial experience that would take great effort or intense concentration to reach, but it's quite normal and requires no more effort than hav-

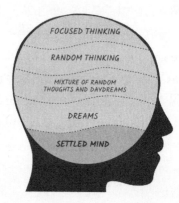

ing a dream while taking a nap. In the settled-mind zone, the pure bliss becomes so great that the thinking process spontaneously comes to a halt. In terms of awareness, the settled state is the deepest state achievable through meditation. The irony is that the meditator is left with little to no awareness that they are achieving it in the moments when they are achieving it.

We'll discuss later how you will know your mind was settled despite the fact that you won't be aware of it in the moment. This may sound like you'll "miss the bliss"—how can you know you were experiencing it if you didn't realize it at the time? But you will know, mainly because of how you will show up *outside* of meditation.

THE CORRECT WAY TO MEDITATE?

When I began dabbling in meditation, one of the instructions I heard repeated, mainly by my yoga teacher peers, was how there is no *correct* way to meditate—meaning there is no way to meditate that works best for everyone. Instead, the meditator should tap into how they are feeling in the moment and practice a meditation technique appropriate to how they feel. There are numerous problems with this philosophy, but the main issue is that saying "there is no correct way to meditate" ignores the cardinal rule of learning any new skill: while there may not be a correct way, there are certainly *best practices* for every skill, and by adhering to those best practices, at least in the beginning, you establish good habits that help you increase both the consistency and reliability of the desired results, as well as your chances of becoming proficient and self-sufficient in the quickest amount of time.

I know about this shortcoming from direct experience with another learned skill that everyone seemed to know how to do but me: swimming. I didn't learn how to swim properly until I was in my thirties. That's not to say I never swam before that. In fact, when I was about ten years old I figured out how to doggy-paddle. And then I learned how to tread water with the peanut-butter-spreading arm motion when I was a teenager. So if I was just frolicking around in the pool, I would be fine, as long as I didn't have to tread for too long. Much more than about a half a minute of treading water, however, and I would go into a full-blown panic.

Now, if you know how to swim, you might think that knowing how to doggy-paddle and tread water provided me with a good base to learn the rest. But I'm proof that truly swimming—moving your arms and legs in sync—is not as intuitive as it may appear, particularly if you didn't put the movements together until you were an adult, like me. My inefficiencies in swimming were embarrassingly exposed while on vacation one summer in Hawaii.

I found myself in a once-in-a-lifetime dream situation, hiking with a buddy of mine (who happened to be an expert swimmer) and four beautiful women along the gorgeous coastline of Maui. We arrived at a volcanic rock overlooking the Pacific Ocean, and one of the women suggested that we strip down to our birthday suits and dive into the sea for a swim around the bend, which meant jumping off the jagged rock we were standing on into choppy ocean water, and navigating around to the other side—at least fifteen hundred feet of ocean swimming. Because the rock stood about ten feet above sea level, once I jumped in, there was no way to get back out. I would be committed. Obviously, I had a major dilemma.

Meanwhile, my buddy couldn't get his clothes off fast enough, and within seconds everyone was diving into the ocean, leaving me behind, topless, shoulders slumped, visualizing the horror and embarrassment of needing to be rescued by one of the women while naked and drowning. As I watched them all swim like dolphins away from the rock, I yelled out over the thunder-clap of the unforgiving waves that I would "stay back to watch our clothes." Even though there was no one around for miles, this was the least emasculating excuse I could think of. Then I quietly vowed to never allow myself to be in that situation again. In fact, my buddy still teases me about it to this day: "Hey, Light, why don't you stay back and, uh, watch our clothes?" The first thing I did upon returning home to Los Angeles was to go down to the local community pool and sign up for some basic swimming lessons.

Cut to me on my first day of swim class, surrounded in the West Hollywood city pool by children of all ages who were also learning to swim. The coach instructed me to swim the length of the pool to assess my abilities. I didn't want to embarrass myself by needing *her* to jump in and save me on my first lesson, so I pleaded for her to just teach me under the assumption that I didn't know anything at all. But she insisted.

Reluctantly I waded into the shallow end, held my breath, pushed off the wall, and started flapping my arms and legs in my best impression of a swimmer. I had no idea what I was doing. And after no more than ten meters, all of my energy was spent, I was taking in water, my chest was on fire, and my life began passing before my eyes. In a panic, I clutched and clawed my way through what felt like an ocean over to the side of the pool and held on for dear life, as if I had just completed an Ironman competition in record time.

"Okay, good," my new coach said with a reassuring smile, as if she'd just witnessed me cross the Ironman finish line. "Let's start from the beginning."

She got me out of the pool and started teaching me the fundamentals. She showed me how to elongate my body, how to kick my legs, how to twist from side to side so that I could breathe in the water properly. In short, she was teaching me the pieces I'd need to put together to swim freestyle. Then she drilled me over the next several lessons until each individual skill became second nature.

For me this course was revolutionary, and completely changed my relationship with water. Over the first month, I began to learn how to move in concert with the water instead of fighting it. I noticed that whenever I fought the water, it became my enemy, slowing me down and threatening to drown me. But when I practiced lengthening my body, extending my arms, breathing and moving with less effort, the water instantly became friendlier and would assist me as I glided across to the other side. If I stopped moving altogether, the water would support me gently while I caught my breath. If I fought, the water would turn and immediately begin to sink me.

Before long, I was able to swim effortlessly from one side of the pool to the other side. As I mastered the fundamentals, my decades-long panic around large bodies of water transformed into delight. After another month or so of practice, I was finally getting it—*do less to accomplish more.*

Swimming requires repetition more than anything else. There's so much to remember initially, but after you swim a thousand laps, you get out of your head, stop analyzing everything, and start moving with maximum efficiency and effectiveness. I couldn't believe it. Something that had eluded me my entire life now seemed as natural as breathing.

After my swimming training, I could go into a pool and swim a mile with relative ease. I could go into the ocean and swim with confidence. And if I'm in another position to go skinny-dipping off a volcanic rock in Hawaii, I'll be the first one to dive in.

The point is, when it comes to meditation, you are essentially learning how to navigate the thing that every new meditator is deathly afraid of—their thinking mind. Or their busy mind. Or their distracted mind. Or their monkey mind. Or whatever they want to call it. To the untrained meditator, their mind is as scary as that ocean was to me on that day I stood on that jagged rock, looking at the waves crashing, and imagining the worst possible outcome—humiliation, then death by drowning. But if you know how to swim, it doesn't matter how much water is in front of you. If you know how to meditate, it doesn't matter how busy your mind is.

Meditation is *never* about stopping your thoughts, in the same way that swimming is never about stopping the water. Rather, swimming is about learning how to move in concert with the water so you can glide through it and have fun. Likewise, the skill of meditation is about learning how to navigate the contours of the thinking mind so you can glide from the busy focused-thinking zone down into the blissful settled-mind zone.

GO E.A.S.Y. ON YOUR MIND

Any swimming style can get you from one side of the pool to the other. It could be the breaststroke, the backstroke, the butterfly stroke, or the freestyle stroke. The only question is, how hard do you want to work? If you ask any swimmer which of the four main techniques is the easiest to learn and practice for a beginner, most will agree that the freestyle technique is the one you always want to start with. Is the freestyle stroke the only "correct" way to swim? No. Is it the easiest for getting from one side of the pool to the other? Yes. And will it teach you the fundamentals (in this case, the hydrodynamics) for the other strokes? Absolutely.

In the same way, any meditation technique can get you to bliss. But the question is the same: *how hard do you want to work?* What I'm going to show you is not the only meditation technique, nor is it the only "correct" meditation technique, but in my extensive experience, it is by far the easiest technique to begin with, and in practicing it, you will experience bliss (and learn the fundamentals of meditating in the process). It is the meditation equivalent of the freestyle swimming technique. And the key to practicing it is to keep everything easy. *Do less to accomplish more.* To help you remember how to be in meditation, I've created the E.A.S.Y. meditation approach—and now you'll learn what each of those letters stands for.

How to Keep Meditation Feeling E.A.S.Y.

E.A.S.Y is an acronym for the four key principles of the meditation technique. You're going to apply these principles to *all* thoughts, noises, and sensations you experience in meditation— not just the positive ones but the negative ones, too. Each E.A.S.Y. principle will help you form an always-reliable foundation for your daily practice, making meditation feel easy and relaxing. That way you'll reap its many benefits, especially those that occur outside of meditation itself. These principles don't necessarily build upon one another, so don't think of them as progressive.

Instead, call to mind each of the four principles as you become aware of your mind wandering in meditation.

E = EMBRACE

Embrace means you want to practice allowing the existence of *all* of your thoughts and experiences. If you feel like you're dreaming, embrace *all* of your dreams, embrace your sleepiness, all noises, or anything that you previously considered distracting in meditation. Embracing your experiences will help your meditations remain easy, go by very fast, and give you maximum benefit.

A = ACCEPTANCE

Now take embracing one step further: accept. *Acceptance* means that you want to cultivate an attitude that *whatever* is happening in your meditation is what should be happening. That includes happy thoughts, sad thoughts, negative thoughts, sleep, dreams, wondering about the time, and feeling antsy. No need to resist or reject any of those thoughts.

S = SURRENDER

Surrender is another directive that implies embracing and accepting, but it refers specifically to your expectations. In other words, be willing at all times to surrender your idea of how you feel your meditation *should* be progressing. You ideally don't want to be locked into an agenda of "This is what I should be experiencing in meditation." Instead, you want to practice surrendering to whatever thoughts, sensations, noises, or distractions are happening in the moment.

Y = YIELD

Yield complements the principles of embrace, accept, and surrender. It's so important to be open to whatever is happening in your meditation. As you'll see, yielding is easier said than done. If you've tried and failed at meditation, it's likely because you've been conditioned to do the exact opposite of the E.A.S.Y. approach. Think about what we've been trained to believe it takes to be successful in most life endeavors: working hard, control, focus, diligence, remembering important information. That indoctrination will inevitably show up in your process and make your meditations feel hard and clunky. So whenever you catch yourself attempting to control your mind in meditation, remember to return to your E.A.S.Y. approach, and yield to whatever else is happening in your experiences.

By following these four principles, your meditation will go from this experience, where your mind feels trapped in the busy surface zone of focused thinking . . .

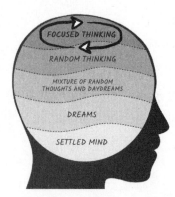

... to this experience, where your mind becomes progressively de-excited, until it becomes settled.

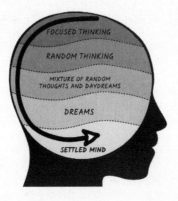

In order for the E.A.S.Y. approach to work even better, you need one more thing to assist in your meditation process—a simple tool I'll reveal in the next chapter. (Hint: You already have it in your possession. Now it's time to understand how exactly to put it to use.)

Timing Your Meditations

If you have been struggling to tame your monkey mind, you may have tried to solve the problem by just meditating more. After all, practice makes perfect, right? Well, in the case of the E.A.S.Y. approach to meditation, overmeditating is as detrimental as *overmedicating*, particularly if you are feeling like you're constantly battling your busy mind.

The optimal dose of the E.A.S.Y. approach to meditation is a minimum of ten minutes and a maximum of twenty minutes, and no more than twice a day. If you meditate twice, space the two sessions about five to seven hours apart. You may want to do a twenty-minute meditation in the morning, upon awakening, and then sit for a fifteen-minute meditation later in the afternoon or early evening. Try to avoid meditating right before bed. It's okay if you do meditate late at night every now and again, but the E.A.S.Y. approach to meditation is designed to boost energy, and if you get in the habit of meditating too late, too often, it could keep you up at night. However, if you follow these instructions and meditate at the recommended times, you should begin sleeping more deeply.

If you have other meditation practices that are different from the approach in this book, consult with your teacher to see how often you should practice them while also practicing what I'm teaching you. But try not to blend the techniques. Blending meditation techniques is like blending medications. The results may be suboptimal.

The reason I'm harping on not overmeditating is that this meditation is going to feel so easy and enjoyable that you'll be tempted to meditate all the time. But trust the process and just stick to one to two meditations per day.

3

YOUR SETTLING SOUND

Wanting to move beyond a busy mind in meditation is not a new endeavor. In India, generations of sages and gurus have spent many millennia researching, developing, and refining technology specifically designed to "settle" the busy human mind. Historically, the Indians were the first to use sound vibrations as a tool for settling the mind. Collectively, these sounds have been referred to as mantras. But not all mantras are created equally, in the sense that they each have distinct and seemingly contradictory purposes.

Think of mantras like unlabeled white pills in a pharmacy. To the untrained eye, they may all look alike. But to a pharmacist the pills are not at all the same—they have drastically different applications and therapeutic properties. If you need an antibiotic and the pharmacist gives you a pill that looks just like the antibiotic but is actually for enhancing sexual performance, the medication won't have the desired effect—though it may leave you confused about why you feel so aroused even though you are on your deathbed with a raging fever and a sinus infection! Some mantras are meant to be sung, some to be thought and repeated silently, some chanted in coordination with your breathing, and some to be whispered to yourself. It just depends on where you got the mantra and what it is meant to be used for.

There are mantras designed for all kinds of purposes: boosting courage, cooking food, aligning the energy centers of the body, improving sleep quality. There are also mantras specifically used for settling the mind in meditation—and this is the category we're interested in—what I call "Settling Sounds."

The Settling Sound I recommend using for the E.A.S.Y. approach to meditation is "ah-hum," pronounced "ah" (like you're sticking your tongue out, saying "Ahhhhh") and "hum" (as in humming a tune to yourself). "Ahhhh-huuummmm."

The Anatomy of the Settled Mind

Settling sounds don't work on the level of literal meaning or religious significance (in Sanskrit, *ah-hum* happens to mean "I am," as in "I am totality"). Instead they are chosen and used for their vibrational qualities. "Ah-hum" offers a vibration that, under the right conditions and used properly, can help even the busiest mind settle with ease.

Believe it or not, you've already had settled-mind experiences several times in your life. Usually they've occurred unintentionally. For instance, have you ever been reading in bed late at night, then you get to a paragraph and . . . time goes by, and you have to reread that paragraph. *Wait, I just read that. Let me reread it.* Then more time goes by and you are still stuck on that same paragraph. *Wait, I'll reread it again.* You try it again (and maybe again) and realize you even forgot what book you were reading: *Where was I?* Maybe it was just for a split second, but you've unintentionally experienced a settled mind, because that's what it feels like.

A settled mind consists of random, unpredictable, and often unintentional time lapses, or gaps in between your thoughts, along with a slight-to-heavy feeling of forgetfulness. Usually when this happens late at night while you're reading or watching television, it indicates that it's time to close your book or turn off your television and go to sleep. In other words, your mind and body are naturally settling into the sleep state of consciousness. A settled mind, whether in sleep or in meditation, is a rested mind. And, as you'll experience very quickly, mental rest is the basis for feeling more physically energized outside of meditation.

By using the Settling Sound "ah-hum" to start your meditations, you'll gradually condition your mind to naturally settle in a more reliable, consistent manner. In the process, you will likely notice some of the same symptoms that you experienced by accident while reading or watching television late at night, including forgetfulness, time lapses, feelings of sleepiness, dreaminess, and gaps in your thinking. As you're going to learn, these are *all* positive symptoms in meditation as well, and they indicate that your mind and body are indeed *settling*.

I first understood the potential relationship between words, sounds, and vibration after watching the 2004 documentary *What the Bleep Do We Know!?*, which highlighted the work of a Japanese scientist, Dr. Masaru Emoto. Dr. Emoto spent over ten years studying the alchemy of water crystals under the influence of nonphysical stimuli (words and thoughts).

According to Dr. Emoto, water is the most receptive of the four elements, so he tested the vibrational effect of different qualities of words on water crystals. What he found was that attaching "high-vibration" words like "love" and "thank you" to bottles of distilled water left out overnight created beautiful, bright, symmetrical water crystals. When he exposed that same water to "low-vibration" words like "hate" and "fear," the crystals began to reform into murky, distorted shapes. Dr. Emoto's work has been cited by many in Western science as being inconclusive, so let's look at the more conventional example of sympathetic vibration. Some music teachers often use sympathetic vibration to demonstrate how sound waves can travel invisibly between any and all objects that "resonate" with a particular vibration. For instance, if someone strikes the E-major chord on a piano, and there are other stringed instruments (such as a violin, harp, or guitar) close by, the E string on each of those instruments will begin to simultaneously vibrate. Essentially, anything in the vicinity that resonates with the E vibration will hum.

Your Settling Sound is a sound that resonates with thoughts that reside below the focused-thinking zone (see the illustration on page 59). Like a mental magnet, the act of thinking the Settling Sound will spontaneously attract your mind away from focused thinking and toward the settled-mind zone—and in doing so, your mind will become increasingly more settled, as opposed to staying in the busy focused-thinking zone, where the other less resonant thoughts and sounds reside.

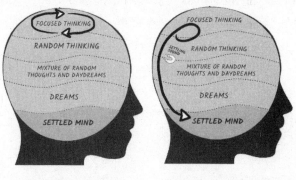

Without a Settling Sound   With a Settling Sound

Most people associate mantras with chanting, focusing, or anchoring, but you won't be doing any of that with your Settling Sound. Instead, you'll practice using it in an almost passive, nonchalant manner. As you perceive the sound "ah-hum" passively in your meditations, it will create an inner form of "white noise," which is what produces a gradual settling effect on your mind and body toward a deeper state of relaxation.

How to Use the Settling Sound

While meditating, you don't want to chant or focus on the word "ah-hum," and you also don't want to repeat it too fast or loud. Instead, practice *whispering* it slowly, while elongating the two syllables, so it sounds more like "aaaaaaaaaah-huuuuummmmm." You can repeat it on your own a few times, and try to feel the subtle vibration as you stretch out the sound.

"Aaaaaaaaaah-huuuuummmmm"

"Aaaaaaaaaah-huuuuummmmm"

"Aaaaaaaaaah-huuuuummmmm"

Then try repeating it just as a whisper:

"Aaaaaaaaaah-huuuuummmmm"

"Aaaaaaaaaah-huuuuummmmm"

"Aaaaaaaaaah-huuuuummmmm"

"Aaaaaaaaaah-huuuuummmmm"

"Aaaaaaaaaah-huuuuummmmm"

"Aaaaaaaaaah-huuuuummmmm"

Next, start to whisper it so softly that if someone was sitting close by, they might be able to see your lips moving, but they wouldn't be able to hear what you were saying:

"Aaaaaaaaaah-huuuuummmmm"

"Aaaaaaaaaah-huuuuummmmm"

"Aaaaaaaaaah-huuuuummmmm"

Finally, close your eyes and passively think the sound to yourself five to ten more times, without vocalizing it or moving your mouth.

Did you notice that your Settling Sound started syncing up to your natural breathing rhythm? If so, this is very common, and it's a sign that you're thinking the sound with the perfect tone and cadence—just slowly and softly enough for it to be barely perceptible, even to you. If that didn't happen, or if you didn't notice it one way or the other, then it's still fine, as long as you practiced it.

When you're ready, try a five-minute practice meditation with the Settling Sound. To do so, close your eyes, and just *think* the

Settling Sound to yourself. Make sure you're sitting comfortably. You'll need a watch or a clock to track your time, or you can set a soft alarm for five minutes. After that, slowly open your eyes. Go ahead and practice it now.

Although five minutes is a relatively short practice, hopefully, you felt more settled (rested) by the end of it. If not, don't worry. Using the Settling Sound gets increasingly easier (and becomes more effective) with practice. And if you did get relaxed, this is only the beginning—there's a lot more of that relaxing feeling to come.

If you heard noises or if you had unrelated or random thoughts while you were passively thinking your Settling Sound, that's actually a good sign of correct practice and pacing. Oftentimes your Settling Sound will fade away completely and you'll simultaneously get lost in one of those other random thoughts. So if that happened, you were also meditating correctly.

In future meditations, if you have to cough, sneeze, or clear your throat, behave as though you were watching TV. In other words, don't think twice about it. Just be natural. If you get itchy, go ahead and scratch. At certain points during your meditation, you will get lost in unrelated thoughts beyond your Settling Sound. Once you realize it, just begin thinking "ah-hum" again as a whispery thought.

Expect your Settling Sound to also fade away during portions of your meditation. And when you notice that it's gone, just passively return to thinking it again. If it continues to disappear, and you notice it, don't feel frustrated, as if you're doing something wrong. Just quietly come back to it. In a typical meditation, you will only be aware of the Settling Sound in spurts—thirty seconds here, a minute there, with random thoughts in between.

Practice Your Settling Sound: A Ten-Minute Meditation

Continue to practice with your Settling Sound, and if you notice that it disappeared, just passively return to thinking it again. Go for ten minutes this time. As before, you can either eyeball the time using a clock or a watch or set a soft alarm for ten minutes. Sit comfortably with back support. Next, close your eyes, and after some time passes, start thinking "aaaaaaaaaah-huuummm" to yourself, very passively. Keep mentally repeating it softly, and as it disappears, just nonchalantly return to thinking it, as if you did nothing wrong. At the end of the ten minutes, you can slowly open your eyes.

How Should I Exit My Meditations?

After you notice that the time is up, say to yourself, "Meditation's over," and rest with your eyes closed for a minute or two. If you want to, use this time to visualize when and where you'll sit for your next meditation. You can also spend that time simply relaxing. If you're tired, let your head gently fall back and rest for a couple of minutes before transitioning back into action. Or, if you're sleepy, lie down and take a nap.

I hope that meditation is feeling easier and more restful. If not, you may be using too much effort while thinking the Settling Sound. Either way, I want you to continue practicing being passive with the Settling Sound. Now, let's go over some common concerns.

What if I don't want to use a Settling Sound to meditate?

If you're brand-new to meditation, in the interest of ease and simplicity, I *highly* recommend following all of the instructions as presented, including using the sound "ah-hum." Think of these instructions like learning how to swim. They may feel awkward at first, but these are the best practices for ultimately enjoying the meditation experience. Over time, you will find meditating in this way very easy. By not using the Settling Sound, you risk making the process unnecessarily hard for yourself.

What if my Settling Sound reminds me of something very unsettling when I think of it?

That happens from time to time. For whatever reason, a person's Settling Sound might remind them of an ex-lover, a traumatic experience, or another negative sensation. But it is possible to overcome this resistance if you weigh the benefits of meditation against any discomfort with the sound itself. The shape and color of my car key reminds me of a large insect, and large insects aren't the most relaxing visual. But without my car key, I can't drive my vehicle and get to the places I want to go, and the larger purpose of traveling with freedom outweighs my preference for a more aesthetically pleasing key.

In the case of disliking the Settling Sound, remember that meditation will ultimately help you achieve a greater state of mental and physical freedom, along with less anxiety and more bliss—well worth any temporary dissatisfaction with the sound itself. With regular use, negative associations eventually fade. Remember, the Settling Sound operates on vibration, not meaning or association. If you prefer a more personalized sound, you can study with a teacher who is trained in assisting meditators to find their own unique Settling Sounds.

Is the Settling Sound the same as a mantra?

While the Settling Sound would technically be considered a mantra, not all mantras would be considered Settling Sounds.

Can I use the mantra I received from my meditation or yoga teacher in place of the Settling Sound?

If you received a personalized mantra from an expert meditation teacher—a mantra that is specific to *you*—then you may substitute it for "ah-hum." I don't recommend that you switch back and forth, as that becomes a distraction in itself. Make a decision about which one you're going to use, and stick with it.

Can I find a meaningful word or mantra online, or an affirmation, and use it instead of the Settling Sound?

Words, sounds, and affirmations you find through the Internet may not have the same deep effect as the Settling Sound "ah-hum" (because of its valuable vibrational properties), and for that reason I would advise against using a sound you find online. Not all mantras are used in the same way, or for the same reason, and as mentioned before, there's usually a specific way you're taught to experience each type of mantra for optimal results. (Remember the medication analogy—all white pills are not the same.)

Can I use my breath instead of "ah-hum"?

It is possible to use your breathing. But the biggest problem with employing the "notice your breath" technique is that most people find that they start trying to control their breath in the process. That kind of conscious control is not going to lead to settling; it can create uneven and sometimes forced breathing! If you do want to notice your breath instead of using the Settling Sound, remember that you don't need to inhale or exhale any deeper than normal, and you can use mouth or nostril breathing. Try to just passively notice your breath. At points while noticing your breathing, you may lose awareness of the fact that you're breathing (in the same way that you may lose awareness of your Settling Sound). When you realize it, just slowly and gently begin to notice your breathing again.

What if I keep overmeditating? Is that okay?

Every now and again, your mind will become so settled that you'll accidentally go over the recommended twenty-minute time frame, and may not realize it until thirty or forty minutes have flown by. It's fine when this happens, but don't *plan* to overmeditate. Overmeditating is when you are purposely meditating with your Settling Sound past twenty minutes. Once the twenty minutes are over, just say to yourself, "Meditation's over," and discontinue use of your Settling Sound.

As you may have noticed, "correct" practice can seem counterintuitive, especially when it includes symptoms like "disappearing," "losing awareness," and "falling asleep." But resisting these natural occurrences is precisely what makes meditation clunky and unenjoyable.

Next we'll examine how virtually all your thoughts can also play a crucial role in the enjoyment of your meditation experiences—and, particularly, how having a lot of unrelated (random) thoughts can actually assist you in your attempt to meditate with success, as long as you remember to be E.A.S.Y. with them.

How to Tell if You're Meditating Correctly

If any of the following occurred during meditation, you were practicing correctly:

- Your Settling Sound disappeared multiple times
- You got lost in unrelated thoughts
- At certain points, you lost track of time
- You felt like you were falling asleep or resting deeply
- You lost awareness of your body

You may have been working too hard if:

- Your Settling Sound felt loud and forceful
- Your meditation seemed to drag on forever
- You sat up completely straight the entire time, instead of sitting comfortably with back support
- You were breathing deeply (like Darth Vader)
- You fought off sleep

4

ALL ROADS LEAD TO ROAM

Forcing yourself to focus for long stretches of time, attempting to push your thoughts away, or trying to manipulate your mind in any way during meditation violates what I refer to as the Roam Principle.

Engaging in the Roam Principle means you willingly and enthusiastically allow your mind to roam through the various threads of thoughts you experience in meditation, and there are no thoughts that are off limits. In meditation, the mind's natural tendency is to roam (drift, wander) from one thought to another, without restraint. Embrace this tendency and meditation will work for you and feel progressively easier. Fight it, and you will feel like you have to work hard in order to meditate. By allowing your mind to roam freely, you will significantly increase the chances of your mind reaching the settled-thinking zone, where it can experience pockets of silence. And banning your mind from roaming at *any* point in meditation will sabotage the desired results. Fighting your roaming mind in order to reach a place of inner bliss in meditation is the equivalent of the swimmer fighting the water while trying to swim across a pool—something that can only ever lead to drowning. Just as the swimmer looks forward to being immersed in the water, the meditator should look forward to being immersed in her thoughts.

The natural tendency of the mind is to roam like a curious little child wandering throughout the house with no particular destination in mind, just pulling things out of drawers, making a mess, getting into the kitchen cabinets and other places parents may not want them to go. By allowing your mind to roam in this indiscriminate fashion, you increase the chances of your mind settling into the pure bliss state, where it will eventually fall silent.

Most people who aren't aware of the roaming tendency of the mind assume that their mind is being "mischievous" and "unruly" when it pulls out and analyzes old dark thoughts that have been hidden away (or so we thought) for years or even decades. They assume that meditation shouldn't include any random or negative thoughts, and the tendency is to try to hide them as quickly as possible. But like the toddler who empties out the junk drawer, the mind is merely being curious—curious enough to roam around to see if there is anything new or interesting to explore.

You may be tempted to use this roaming mind concept as an excuse to *not* meditate. You may not want to have to sit there and think about all of your psychological baggage. But having those kinds of thoughts is actually an indication of correct practice, and will ultimately leave you in a more blissful position mentally, physically, and emotionally. (More on this in Chapter 11, where I discuss the four types of thoughts you will have in meditation, and why they occur.)

And think of it this way: trying to discipline your mind in meditation is about as effective as trying to ban the curious child from being curious. You can't will away the natural curiosity of a young mind, even if you declare certain areas off-limits. If anything, restricting access will just make a child more determined to discover what you're trying to hide. Seasoned meditators understand that a wandering, curious mind should be embraced and celebrated—never cursed.

The Art of Being Passive

I admit, learning how to allow the mind to roam is easier said than done. In fact, I would label it as an art—like learning how to put the spin on a bowling ball as you release it down the lane, or mastering the plié in ballet. It reminds me of the "questions game," which my friends and I used to play in college.

The object of the questions game seems ridiculously simple (at first): to answer one question with another question. To play, you gather five or six friends in a circle, and one person starts it off by asking someone else a question. The rule is, whenever someone in the circle looks at you and asks you a question, you then have to quickly ask someone else a new question. What you're *not* supposed to do is answer the question you're being asked. If you accidentally answer the question or make a statement, you're out of the game. Everyone else keeps playing until it gets down to the last two people, firing questions back and forth at each other. Inevitably, one of them will stumble, and the last person remaining is crowned the winner.

The game is deceptively challenging because we don't realize how much it is in our nature to not only pay attention to what's being asked of us but then respond accordingly, even if the question is complete nonsense . . . *especially* if it's nonsense. You see it all the time in the questions game, particularly if the question you're being asked is offensive. But the key to winning is passivity—to train yourself to completely ignore the question that you've just been asked and instead to place your attention on asking your next random question. In other words, you want to master the art of remaining process-oriented (calmly thinking of your next question) instead of allowing yourself to be outcome-oriented (letting someone trick you into answering by listening to and considering their personal or offensive question). After practicing this unique skill many times, a seasoned questions game player learns to tune out the nonsense spouting from everyone's mouth while passively thinking up their next random question.

Can you spot the correlation with the Roam Principle? As the mind roams through the occasional nonsense (including negative thoughts), we're naturally tempted to respond to it, get mad about it, repress it, understand it, or try to control it in some way! But in order to succeed in meditation, you must train yourself to be E.A.S.Y. and remain passive in order to allow your mind to roam through any negative or pleasant thoughts and toward the settled-mind zone.

You cannot control or manipulate your mind into a settled state. As with the questions game, you are never in control of what the other players ask you. A clever questions game player is going to occasionally hit below the belt and ask questions that feel hurtful in order to throw you off, such as "When are you going to get your life together?" or "Why do you eat so much?" If those kinds of thoughts occur in meditation, you must become like Gandhi and practice passive resistance. In other words, *any* reaction other than remaining cool, calm, and completely passive under fire violates the Roam Principle and will only make the meditation feel harder. As I promised in the last section, we'll deal with why we occasionally have negative thoughts in Part Two, but for now, practice not letting them bug you in your meditations. Whenever they come, just think: "Ah, the questions game," and passively return to your Settling Sound.

Meditating on a Dimmer Switch

As your mind begins roaming in the direction of becoming increasingly more settled, you're going to experience a series of thoughts, such as:

"*I'm meditating . . . ahhhh-huuummmm . . .*"

"*I need to change my toothbrush . . . ahh-humm . . .*"

"*I should switch jobs, too, while I'm at it . . . ahh-humm . . .*"

"*I always wanted to be an architect . . .*"

"*The sound of the ocean is so soothing . . .*"

"*Harry Potter . . .*"

"*Flying . . . like a bird . . .*"

"*Higher . . . higher . . .*"

Think of this process like a dimmer switch. In other words, you start with the awareness that you're meditating turned all the way up (100 percent), then as you begin the Settling Sound, your awareness drops incrementally, to 75 percent, then to only 50 percent, and so on, all the way down to maybe 10 percent or even 0 percent awareness. Chances are you won't notice that you're losing awareness until *after* you've already lost it. It's like falling asleep at night. If you're lying in your bed thinking about how badly you want to be sleeping, you may inadvertently keep yourself awake. Falling asleep means not being aware that you're falling asleep.

Similarly, if an actual dimmer switch is being gradually turned down from 100 percent to 90 percent, there will be little difference to the naked eye. It may even feel like the light is still turned all the way up. If the light continues to be turned down, you may still barely notice it. But if the light is at 60 percent brightness and then it suddenly gets turned up to 100 percent brightness, you would notice that 40 percent difference in brightness right away.

The loss of awareness in meditation is gradual. It's not fast, linear, or exclusive. By that I mean you can lose awareness that you're meditating, while passively thinking your Settling Sound, while being aware of background noises, and while getting lost in your everyday thoughts, all at the same time—like a lava lamp of activity. In fact, the more unrelated elements you experience while meditating the better, because *it means you're becoming less aware that you're meditating.*

As you may have experienced already, you will get lost in all manner of thoughts—both positive and negative. You'll have amazing ideas, visions of the future, intuitive hits, solutions to problems, and the like. But you could also experience many thoughts related to hardships and challenges at your job, in your relationship, or with your children, as well as thoughts about failures, self-judgment, loathing, hate, and romance; song lyrics, movie plots, and book titles; noise, sounds, distractions, and itches. Really, anything else you've *ever* thought about outside meditation can potentially bubble up *inside* meditation. Regardless, it's not the content of your thoughts that tells you where you are in the meditation, *it's the amount of awareness you have.* See the following illustration:

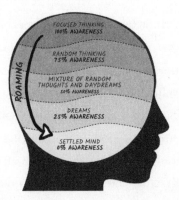

Because you're the one getting lost in the experience, and it's *your* awareness that's decreasing incrementally, you will never know that you are losing awareness. The only thing you may be aware of are the thoughts you're getting lost in, as they become less focused and more dream-like. At some point around 25 percent awareness, you'll be experiencing mostly dream-like thoughts, which basically feels like you're dreaming. This is where you may experience thoughts related to strange colors, shapes, bizarre sensations, or anything else that may make you wonder (after the fact), "What did that mean?"

It's very similar to the feeling we have with nighttime dreams, where we don't know we're dreaming *while* we're dreaming. It's not until we wake up that we realize we were in a dream. And when we share the story of our dream, we usually make the following disclaimer: "It was *strange*" or "It was *weird*." Though it probably made complete sense while we were having the dream, no one ever woke up and announced, "I just had the most logical dream!" A *logical* dream is an oxymoron. What compels us to share our dream is not necessarily what happened in the dream, but how it made us feel. In meditation, there's no need to interpret our thoughts or dreams, no matter how weird, random, normal, surface, or subtle.

As you continue to practice your Settling Sound, you'll begin to notice how your awareness level fluctuates between being fully aware (focused), partially aware (random thoughts), and not being aware at all (settled mind). Over time you may spot trends, where you have the most awareness in the beginning of your meditation and the least awareness near the end of your meditation. But no matter what happens, understand that with consistency, the trends will shift and morph, and the best way to treat the experience is to practice accepting whatever is happening in the moment as correct.

THOUGHT SHAMING

NO MORE "THOUGHT SHAMING"

We covered "position shaming" in Chapter 1. But there's another kind of shaming that is tempting in meditation: "thought shaming." I think of thought shaming as the practice of making critical, potentially discouraging comments about the frequency or content of thoughts during meditation. An example of thought shaming is telling yourself in meditation that you are having "too many thoughts." Another example of thought shaming is when a meditation guide instructs you to "let go" of negative thoughts.

There's a famous quote attributed to Johnny Depp's Captain Jack Sparrow character from *The Pirates of the Caribbean*: "The problem is not the problem. The problem is your attitude about the problem." The same is true for meditation. A dismissive or negative attitude toward the mind during meditation will have one natural outcome: it will spike the activity in your mind, keeping it trapped in the busy focused-thinking zone, where you will remain hyperaware of the fact that you're meditating. The E.A.S.Y. approach flips the thinking process away from judge and jury and into a *celebration*. But this requires you to adopt the opposite attitude of thought shaming, and practice thought embracing, accepting, surrendering, and yielding, no matter the content. This approach will feel counterintuitive at first, because thought shaming is so rampant in the meditation world that we accept it as proper technique. But you will slowly be able to expose the misconception that random thoughts in meditation are bad as you practice adjusting your attitude about your mind accordingly—it's noble and supportive, not obstructive or mischievous.

When you sit to meditate and close your eyes, you want to begin with the understanding that this experience is going to involve *a lot* of thinking—just like the skydiver knows the experience of jumping from a plane is going to involve a lot of wind and the ocean swimmer knows that being in the water is going to involve a lot of wetness. In order to enjoy the experience of meditation, you must make an agreement with yourself that incessant thinking is a positive outcome, not a negative one. After all, it's not the content of your thoughts that matter; it's how you handle them. Do you embrace them or resist them? Those two approaches will yield vastly different results.

Furthermore, instead of wishing and hoping for nice thoughts instead of bad thoughts, you must practice enthusiastically *embracing any and all thoughts*—whatever they are, no matter the content. That's the attitude that pro meditators have in meditation. Amateur and untrained meditators mistakenly enter into meditation like soldiers going into battle, determined to fight their mind with the heavy artillery of their ironclad will. But this is an exercise in futility. The mind is both David and Goliath. And it always wins that battle. Always. Still unconvinced?

Put It to the Test: To Shame or Not to Shame, That Is the Question

Don't take my word for it. During your next meditation, try testing the two different approaches for yourself. First, for ten minutes, try as best as you can to quiet your mind. Use your Settling Sound aggressively. Use intense focus. Go ahead and thought-shame yourself to death. Then, for the last ten minutes, embrace *everything*. Be passive with your Settling Sound, and celebrate all thoughts—no matter the content. And see for yourself which ten minutes feel better and fly by faster.

TIME FLIES WHEN YOUR MIND IS ROAMING

If I were to ask you to stare at a blank wall for twenty minutes straight, it would feel a lot longer than twenty minutes, wouldn't you agree? Maybe even two or three times longer? (You don't actually have to run this experiment—just use your imagination.)

The reason time slows down in that situation is that you would be aware of what you were doing (staring at a wall) for pretty much the entire time. And whenever we're 100 percent aware of anything (focused thinking), the time *always* feels longer than when we're lost in the moment (random thinking). The awareness of time is an important cue to remember, because it will be your one true gauge of whether or not your mind was settling in your meditation. In almost every instance, when you're on track, you'll find that time will seem to speed up. And if you're off track (because you're thought shaming, working too hard, or focusing too much), time crawls along painfully slowly.

It's the loss of awareness that causes time to feel like it's speeding up in meditation. For example, if you meditate for twenty minutes and reach a point where you only have 25 percent awareness, the entire twenty-minute experience may feel as short as only ten minutes, which means you emerge from that meditation having sat for a full twenty minutes but only remember about ten minutes' worth of thoughts. For the other ten minutes, you don't remember anything. That is because your mind was more settled than you realized. See the following chart:

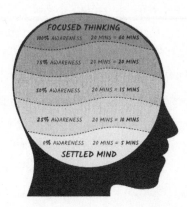

This is good news, because it means that anytime a twenty-minute meditation feels shorter than one hour, you were moving toward having a more settled mind. In other words, whenever you notice that the meditation time felt shorter than it would've been if you were staring at a wall, you have hard evidence that your mind was indeed settling, despite what you thought about during meditation. If you're still unsure that anything positive was happening, then again, don't take my word for it. Go stare at a wall for real; try doing so for twenty minutes and see how long that feels compared to your meditation.

WHAT MAKES MEDITATION H.A.R.D.

At this point, it should be clear that the goal of meditation is *not* to have a quiet mind 100 percent of the time. To my knowledge, no one in the history of meditation has been able to force their mind into silence, and certainly no householder has accomplished that feat. Instead, the goal is to reframe the mistaken notion that thinking in meditation is a symptom of incorrect practice. So instead of berating your mind, you understand its nature, and knowing how to meditate in concert with the mind's nature, you increase your chances of having a more blissful experience. This means that some portions of your meditations will feel more settled than others. But either way, you will have a practice that you look forward to doing every day.

Let's outline some very common mistakes that can make your meditation experiences incredibly H.A.R.D., no matter how well-intentioned or experienced you are. Following each mistake, I offer recommended adjustments to help you replace the unsustainable habit with a new one.

H = HOLDING YOUR POSITION

Many times we associate meditation with sitting like a monk and being completely still. If you have to scratch an itch, you resist it. If you have to shift your position due to your leg falling asleep, you try to will the discomfort away. But if you take this rigid approach to meditation, your body will remain uncomfortable, which will keep your mind active, and that will make your experiences feel unnecessarily difficult.

Recommended adjustment: No matter what happens, remain completely relaxed and fluid in your position. Allow yourself to move, scratch the itches, cough, sneeze, clear your throat, shift in your seated position, swat the fly away, or do whatever else is necessary to remain comfortable.

A = AUSTERITY

Austerity means being stiff or rigid during meditation, and not just in your body, but also in your mind. It means choosing a place to meditate that is uncomfortable, such as on a rock, in cold weather, or even on a meditation cushion. This includes sitting with your back erect and crossing your legs into lotus position if that's not comfortable for you. Unnecessary hand configurations fall into this category as well as trying to focus or concentrate.

Recommended adjustment: Ideally, you want your body *and* your mind to stay as relaxed and malleable as possible in order to maximize the feeling of physical and mental comfort. Always be willing to surrender control or focus during your practice.

R = RESISTANCE

As I've reiterated many times now, thinking is a legitimate part of the meditation process, yet new meditators still mentally exhaust themselves by fighting their thoughts, feeling that *their* thoughts are somehow the exception to the rule. A self-imposed obstacle to your enjoyment of the practice is resisting your thoughts, noises, sleep, or any distractions.

Recommended adjustment: Don't resist anything! You want to practice embracing *all* of your mental experiences, and the physical ones, too (tics, jolts, itches, twitches, noises, etc.).

D = DOUBTING THE PROCESS

The E.A.S.Y. meditation approach is based on ancient householder meditation principles. All you have to do to succeed is follow these basic tenets, and trust the process as you move ahead and become consistent with daily meditation. For readers with some basic meditation experience, the temptation may be to override the native process and start adding in elements from other techniques, with the intention of making it work faster or better. But *this will only result in making the meditation feel harder than necessary.* There is no shortcutting or hacking the E.A.S.Y. process.

Recommended adjustment: I have a name for the practice of re-mixing or blending several meditation techniques into one practice: a Kanye West meditation! My advice? Leave the remixing to Kanye—he's much better at it. But for you, in order to get the best results, follow the process exactly as instructed in this book. I've shown you the foundational principles for achieving success in meditation, so you can remove all of the guesswork, relax into the process, and enjoy the best experiences possible.

A QUICK REVIEW OF YOUR TECHNIQUE

By now you should find the E.A.S.Y. approach to be the most successful way to meditate, simply because it allows the mind to settle by using the least amount of effort. Before we move on, let's review the ten-step process I introduced at the beginning of Part One, to double-check and make sure you're getting the full effect from each meditation you do. And if you're not enjoying meditation yet, I urge you to periodically review these steps and make sure you're still on track:

1. *Always* **sit comfortably.** Find a sofa, chair, car seat, airplane seat, bus seat, church pew, or anywhere you can sit comfortably with your back supported. Ideally, this should also be a place where you're not going to be physically disturbed while meditating.

2. **Use an easy-to-see timing device.** If you're using your phone, it's best to use a digital clock application with an LCD display, as opposed to a timer. Make sure you can see it clearly. You may also use a watch as long as you don't have to squint in order to see the time.

3. **Calculate your finish time** *beforehand.* Meditate no more than twenty minutes. Calculate your finish time at the beginning so you don't have to do the math during your meditation.

4. **Relax first, then ease into your Settling Sound.** After closing your eyes and before starting your Settling Sound, relax your entire body, beginning in your toes, and working your way up toward your head. Then start thinking your Settling Sound passively.

5. **Stay passive with your Settling Sound.** From your physically relaxed state, begin thinking "ahhhhhh-huuuummm" very passively. Don't be surprised if your Settling Sound naturally disappears after you've been passively thinking it for a few minutes. Expect your mind to begin roaming through random thoughts, and/or dreams as your mind begins settling. You may also fall asleep.

6. **Enjoy getting lost.** Correct practice involves frequently losing track of your Settling Sound, and even forgetting that

you're meditating for much of the time. Whenever you realize that it happened, celebrate it (as opposed to feeling regret), and begin passively thinking your Settling Sound again.

7. Stay easy when you realize you're meditating. Remember, there's no time limit between realizing your mind has been roaming (or you drifted off to sleep, or had a settled-mind experience) and passively returning to your Settling Sound.

8. Peek freely and often at the time. You may frequently have the thought "I wonder how long I've been meditating." Each time you have the thought about the time, quickly peek at your clock or watch and verify how much time has passed, even if you're using a soft alarm. It's better to satisfy your curiosity if you're thinking about the time. After glancing, you may calculate that you have five or three minutes remaining, or you may see that you've accidentally overmeditated.

9. Wait a bit before opening your eyes. When you've reached the end, or accidentally surpassed your finish time, keep your eyes closed and continue sitting for another minute or two. Now that meditation is over, there's no need to continue thinking your Settling Sound. Just say to yourself, "Meditation's finished," and continue sitting for a few minutes. Use this time to make a mental appointment with yourself for your next meditation or to just rest.

10. Always come out slowly at the end. Peek at the clock, and after you verify that at least two minutes have passed, close your eyes, take a beat, and then open them slowly. You're done.

THE IDEAL MEDITATION SCHEDULE

Morning meditation routine: Before you meditate in the morning, freshen up in the bathroom. Then find somewhere with privacy to sit for your first meditation of the day. This can be back in your bedroom or elsewhere. Also, try to meditate *before* having breakfast or coffee.

Evening meditation routine: Keep a minimum of five hours in between your morning and evening meditation. For instance, if you meditated at 8:00 a.m., then you can meditate again after 2:00 p.m. For best results, try to meditate on a relatively empty stomach, and if you can, meditate before dinner. If you miss that window, meditate a few hours before bed. And as a last resort, meditate before going to sleep.

Next, we'll review what I refer to as the eleventh step of the technique. This step is often the missing ingredient for not only deepening your enjoyment of meditation and enhancing the overall effectiveness of your daily practice but also for ensuring that meditation makes as big an impact as possible both in your life and in the world at large.

5

THE EXCHANGE PRINCIPLE

Posture, comfort, Settling Sound, surroundings—these are all important aspects for optimizing the process of meditation. But there is one more crucial component in the process, the eleventh step: making an exchange. You might not think of this as a "technique" issue, but making an exchange is as important to the enjoyment of meditation as sitting with back support and adopting a passive attitude. For one thing, your exchange will help to solidify your commitment, and having an ironclad commitment will increase your consistency. Being more consistent will improve your technique, which will lead to more beneficial and enjoyable experiences, and ultimately result in a more fulfilling life.

One time-tested way to instantly increase your commitment and elevate your meditation experiences is to give away something that you hold dear, and to do so in the name of your practice. Confused? Let me tell you about the commitment I made more than fifteen years ago when I began meditating with success.

I remember exactly when my exchange took place: seven o'clock on the second Monday morning in February 2003, twelve hours after I had first laid eyes on the happiest person I'd ever met—my meditation teacher, MV.

. After we'd met him the night before, he asked that all of us who were interested in learning to meditate make a one-time financial contribution equivalent to our average weekly salary. This meant that a heart surgeon earning $5,000 a week would be obliged to pay $5,000 to be trained, while a bus driver making $500 a week could pay $4,500 less to take the same training. He went on to explain that we should each decide for ourselves (on the honor system) how much to contribute. He was not interested in knowing what we did for a living or seeing our tax returns. "Make your exchange in good faith and with your highest integrity," he instructed, "and if there is any doubt as to the correct amount, err on the side of being generous."

He was extraordinarily casual and nonchalant when discussing how the exchange worked, and it didn't seem to matter to him one way or another whether any of us took him up on it. He wasn't so much selling us his services as he was allowing us to determine what personal value *we* might assign to the ancient and transformative practice of meditation as well as to his time and expertise as our teacher for life.

But I didn't share his nonchalance! In fact, I can't recall wanting to learn anything as badly as I wanted to study meditation with MV, and for me the odd request to make such a steep exchange for meditation was what sealed the deal. I came home excited to learn, and took a hard look at the little earnings I made from being a relatively new yoga teacher, which totaled about $200 to $300 per week. I was still trying to make a name for myself, so I accepted teaching jobs anywhere I could for little to no money just to get experience. However, I viewed the exchange as an opportunity to project into "the universe" the amount I desired to make (per week) at that time. So I went to the ATM machine the next morning, held my breath, withdrew $400 of the $900 I had in my account, and dropped the entire stash into a wooden box upon entering for my first day of instruction.

Looking back, I can easily say it was the best $400 I ever spent. If it hadn't been for my exchange—which was nearly half of my entire net worth at the time—I doubt that I would be sitting here in my office writing this book on meditation fifteen years later. Had MV not encouraged me to determine the value of the practice for myself, I probably wouldn't have taken it seriously enough to meditate as instructed and commit to sitting daily, even when I didn't feel like it.

Once I started down the path to becoming a meditation teacher myself, I truly understood why it is ideal for a new meditator to *start* the process by making a meaningful exchange. It's a kind of screen—a test to see who is serious about committing to the practice, as well as an incentive to take the lessons seriously, follow the instructions as provided, do the homework meditation exercises, and ultimately to show up for himself, to stay curious, and to be willing to follow the instructions well enough to get the benefit.

The concept of a fair exchange is the foundation of how we do business. We value and appreciate what we pay for, and we are prone to disregard or undervalue those items and experiences that come to us cheaply or freely. Even though it's free to sit and close our eyes as often as we'd like, the ancient gurus and sages of India have a rich tradition of requiring a meaningful exchange in return for teaching spiritual techniques. It's known as *gurudakshina,* which means "teacher's fee."

Gurudakshina can also be used by the teacher as a test, to see how committed a self-proclaimed seeker is to their own personal growth—which is arguably the most difficult and time-consuming type of growth, and simultaneously the most rewarding. This test may be administered by a simple request: "Give me something." *Gurudakshina* could include money, your car, your time, or even physical labor. Come and scrub my floors. Come and spend time in my ashram in complete silence. Stop eating meat, or stop having sex and become a celibate. Wear a robe. And so on.

On the surface, any one of those demands would seriously raise eyebrows, especially considering that it is merely knowledge that is being received. And the Westerner, not used to making such a premium exchange for spiritual knowledge or physical discomfort, may initially reject the idea that knowledge could be worth more than time, money, temporarily abstaining from sex or meat, or whatever is being asked of them in return. Or they begin bargain-hunting, searching for the best deal, as if spiritual liberation was the same as shopping online for a new television. But any scoffing at the request for *gurudakshina* tells the teacher everything she needs to know about your priorities and the value you place on the knowledge and experience she has to offer you.

Additionally, a teacher may have no personal need for the exchange he is requesting. Oftentimes he is merely testing you, just to see how attached you are to your stuff, your habits, or your fixed ideas about how knowledge should be imparted. Remember the classic Zen parable about the seeker who approaches the master and brags that he has learned from all of the other masters and he now wants to know what this master can teach him. After quiet consideration, the master politely asks the seeker if he would like some tea, and when the seeker agrees, the master begins calmly pouring the tea until it overflows out of the cup. The seeker shouts, "What are you doing? Don't you see the cup is already full?" The master responds, "Yes, and that is why I can't teach you anything until you first empty your cup." *Gurudakshina* is one way for a sincere seeker to "empty her cup."

Do you consider your stuff to be worth more than having a teacher show you how to achieve spiritual liberation? Is it worth more than your commitment to your personal growth and evolution? Are you serious enough about your transformation to follow the instructions as laid out? Are you willing to persevere through the inevitable bumps and pitfalls along the way to mastery? If so, there's a cost to that level of commitment. And it gets determined by you.

Every sincere meditation teacher who has taught long enough learns (usually the hard way) about the importance of requiring a meaningful exchange, whether it be money, time, or some other measure of exchange. You see how much more the student appreciates what they are receiving when they have some skin in the game. The few times I've taught someone to meditate with no exchange, it usually backfired. Many of those students, giving one excuse or another, didn't even have enough of a commitment to stick around until the end of my four-day training. I quickly saw that, while everyone's intentions are generally good in the beginning, by exempting someone from making an exchange, I inadvertently (and regrettably) set them up for failure. Therefore, to ensure your success with meditation, I strongly encourage you to take advantage of the Exchange Principle, deciding upon and swiftly making an exchange that feels meaningful to you.

DETERMINING YOUR EXCHANGE

Without question, making a meaningful exchange at the beginning of your meditation practice will deeply and positively influence your relationship with meditation over the course of your life. There are no scientific studies proving the benefit of making an exchange. But in my own experience, as with the thousands of people I've taught, I've seen firsthand how much more committed a meditator becomes *after* making the exchange. They show up on time. They pay more attention during the training. They ask questions. They meditate even when it's not convenient or when they don't feel like it. They reach out for help if they are struggling. If you begin with a high degree of integrity when it comes to making a meaningful exchange, then I guarantee you that same level of worthiness will be refunded back to you in richer, more elevated experiences both in and out of meditation, and particularly on the days when you may be prone to skip.

You may be wondering, "Hold on, I've already acquired this book, so isn't *that* my exchange?" You're right in that an exchange has taken place, but that's not the type of exchange I'm referring to. I'm specifically referring to a *meaningful* exchange—something that ideally makes you feel a pinch.

The easiest and quickest form of a meaningful exchange is to donate a significant sum of money to a worthy cause. If you're running low on funds, you could donate your time. Or you can offer your professional service to a cause, or create art for a public space. Or you could engage yourself in a series of random acts of giving. Whatever your exchange ends up being, it should be related to something you personally care about, and the exchange should ideally benefit others as well. This doesn't include something you were going to give away anyway, like donating cans of soup that have been sitting in your cupboard for two years, returning money you owed to a friend, or giving clothes you no longer wear to charity. It should be something more precious than that, something that will cause you to even think twice about giving it away.

Your gift can even be anonymous as well. A homeless person can give away a dollar and feel the necessary pinch, whereas a millionaire can donate her precious time over a series of

weekends helping the homeless and that will satisfy her requirement. If it doesn't feel heart-centered and meaningful, then it
doesn't fully satisfy this requirement. And please, don't send
me any checks (my publisher already satisfied my exchange
for this book). Your exchange will be better utilized to benefit
those around you. After all, you're making an exchange for you,
not me.

You may be thinking that not all meditation offerings require
an exchange, or that you know plenty of meditation teachers
who teach for free. If you look closely, there is still an exchange
taking place. It could be in the form of time or attention (for
instance, taking off from work to go away for a ten-day silent
retreat and pledging to stay the entire time no matter what), or it
could involve strengthening your will (by giving up meat, taking
a vow of silence, agreeing to be celibate, or shaving your hair—
all costs of living in a monastery). Elizabeth Gilbert, in *Eat Pray
Love,* described her exchange for meditation as having to spend
her free time on her hands and knees scrubbing the floors of the
ashram.

Try not to view this request as punishment, busywork, or an
obstacle to meditating. It's the opposite. I really want you to succeed at meditation, and when it comes to learning meditation
from a book, the lack of a proper exchange is usually the missing
ingredient for success. I know from lots of experience that your
practice will also work more seamlessly after making a meaningful exchange. So view this exercise as an unexpected and potentially delightful opportunity.

Know that it is also optional, and you can indeed make an exchange later. But if you're inspired to play along now (which is what I strongly recommend), you'll see that everything you give will be refunded back to you in greater amounts than you initially gave—*because you trusted the process.*

Food for Thought

When my sixteen-year-old nephew expressed interest in taking my meditation course, he didn't have much money to exchange, but he felt inspired by the idea of a meaningful exchange. In the end, he decided to make sandwiches for the homeless. He went to the store and bought all of the ingredients with $50 of his own money and spent a couple of hours in the kitchen making the sandwiches, then another hour or so passing them out in an area in Los Angeles with a high concentration of homeless people. His sincere effort satisfied the exchange for his instruction. Younger children who take my training are asked to create a piece of art in exchange for their instruction, which I then display at my studio.

Here are some other ideas for exchanges that may resonate with you:

- Prepare/deliver meals to shut-ins through your church or another community group
- Volunteer to tutor children after school
- Spearhead a drive for back-to-school clothing, food, or school supplies in your community for families in need
- Organize a bake sale or other hands-on event and donate all of the proceeds to charity
- Sign up to become a Big Brother or Big Sister to a young child for a year
- Make time for regular visits with an elderly neighbor

To see more ideas, or to share the story of your exchange, visit blissmore.co.

ASKING THE RIGHT QUESTIONS

A disciple once took on a yearlong residency at his meditation teacher's ashram in a foreign country. Although there was no monetary exchange for his ongoing spiritual teaching from the master, his exchange was to transcribe reels of audio recordings from the master's daily lectures and help to turn them into a book. However, this task coincided with a surprise visit from the disciple's girlfriend, who had recently flown into the country with the hope of spending a few days with him.

Knowing that his girlfriend had gone to great trouble and expense to surprise him, the young man was in a terrible bind. He obviously wanted to spend quality time with her. But the transcription work he was doing was time-sensitive, and he had previously agreed to commit fully to his assigned task and remain free of distraction.

Still, because this was a special circumstance, the young disciple decided to seek special permission from the master, thinking he would make a rare exception just this one time. After all, the man hadn't known his girlfriend was going to surprise him. Surely the master would understand.

However, upon hearing the sincere request, the master nonchalantly reminded the young man of his agreement, and also of the consequence of breaking his commitment. He displayed no sympathy, and warned the man that he was absolutely free to spend as much time as he would like with his girlfriend, but he would no longer be able to continue studying at the ashram, and their teacher-student relationship would effectively come to an end.

Slightly shocked by the master's lack of compassion, the man agreed that he understood his options and requested a few hours to deliberate over what to do: spend time with his girlfriend, or honor the exchange he had made for his spiritual studies with his master.

A few agonizing hours passed. Near the end of a very thought-filled, mind-racing, and emotional meditation, which was full of flashes of how disappointed his girlfriend would be after traveling all that way, the young man's choice crystalized. He calmly returned to the room of the master and waited outside for the invitation to enter. After being called in, he made his announcement: "My beloved teacher, thank you for giving me an opportunity to consider all options. I have made my choice. I will continue my studies with you here at the ashram. This is what I agreed to, and I will honor my agreement. Thank you for helping me remember my priorities."

As the disciple began to turn and walk away, the master said, "One second. That is the choice I thought you would make. I was so sure that you would honor your commitment that I have already arranged to have my driver give you and your girlfriend a tour of the city for the next few days, as well as access to my offsite quarters, along with my staff. It's all at your disposal. Enjoy your time with your girlfriend."

I love this story, because it exemplifies the importance of aligning our priorities for enjoying a full life with our commitment to our practice, with the outcome being better than we initially imagined. Like anyone making a commitment to something bigger than them, there will be temptation to compromise or barter away their resolve in the name of fun, laziness, or to please others. But we don't realize how, by compromising our inner bliss, we're essentially trading something that is worth more than diamonds (our bliss) for another experience that may only be worth the value of an orange (tasty, but ultimately temporary).

If we actively look for excuses not to meditate, we'll find plenty of them. But if we can remember to ask stronger questions, it will lead to better choices. For example, instead of asking, "Is skipping meditation this once going to kill me?" ask, "Is meeting my friends for drinks going to help me stabilize inner bliss, like my meditation practice would?" You get the same answer, but two drastically different choices.

WHY WE STOP

Over the years, I've found that a little more than half the people I've trained to meditate stay fairly consistent in their practice. But we can all occasionally talk ourselves out of engaging in the very behaviors that we know are beneficial for us, whether it's healthier eating, regular exercise, or staying committed to our wellness practices. I know I've personally used weak questions and lame excuses to justify my slacking behavior before. That's how I'm able to identify them so well. And believe it or not, I did it with meditation, too, in the first couple of years after I learned.

Here are the most common excuses I've used myself, or heard over and over from amateur meditators who've rationalized themselves out of a daily meditation practice. And I've included my rebuttals as well.

"I started practicing yoga instead."

Beautiful—meditation can help with yoga, too. In fact, meditation without yoga is still meditation. But yoga without meditation is just exercise.

"Life got hectic, and now I'm waiting for things to get back on track before I start meditating again."

Waiting for life to be distraction-free in order to start meditating again is like waiting to become an expert swimmer before ever going in the water. That's obviously backward, and you're deluding yourself into thinking that your life will spontaneously get better without you making time for your inner work. It's the other way around.

"I keep falling asleep."

That's probably because you're sleep-deprived. Go ahead, allow yourself to fall asleep. That will help you pay off your sleep debt.

"I don't think I'm doing it right."

Meditation is a practice-oriented practice, which means your E.A.S.Y. approach will improve with time. Just practice being passive with everything, and occasionally think your Settling Sound whenever you remember to do so, and that's pretty much it. It's not rocket science.

"It didn't work for me."

I'll bet that's because your expectations were too high and your commitment was too low. Nothing good happens overnight.

Were you consistent? Did you make an exchange? Think of this process like going to the gym. If you never go or if you don't wear the proper clothes, it doesn't mean the gym didn't work. You have all of the tools you need for creating the best experiences a meditation practice can provide. You just have to use them as instructed and give it time. Practice consistently for at least six to nine months, and then you can humor yourself by questioning whether or not meditation is working.

"I don't have time to meditate."

This is one of the most common excuses not to meditate. But what someone really means is they're not being *efficient* enough with their current time and commitments, and they're spending far too much time watching television or scrolling through social media. Bottom line: if the average Westerner can spend more than ten hours a day staring at a screen, you should be able to find ten to twenty minutes a day to meditate. It's like saying you don't have time to brush your teeth or shower. Of course you do. Everyone does.

In short, there are endless excuses for not meditating, but countless reasons why you should (and we'll talk more about that in Part Two). Give me a reason why you can't and I'll give you a reason why you should. (Go ahead, try me. I could play that game all day long.) But, ultimately, only you can make it happen. The key—as with any good habit you are trying to embrace—is consistency. But I've got you covered. Read on.

6

ACHIEVING LIFTOFF: INTEGRATING
MEDITATION INTO YOUR LIFE

When I found out that one of my meditation students was a Cessna pilot, I began bombarding him with the following questions: How high can a Cessna fly? What's the maximum distance a Cessna can travel? How fast do you have to go down the runway to achieve liftoff?

The answer to that last question fascinated me the most. "Ninety miles an hour," he said. Once the Cessna reaches ninety miles an hour, the plane will begin lifting off, whether the pilot wants it to or not. It reminded me of what I'd been telling my students for years about what it takes to achieve "liftoff" in meditation—around three months, or ninety days, of consistency. Many experts say it only takes twenty-one days to form a habit. But I like to have my meditation students hedge their bets and not underestimate the grip stress has on their lives.

As you should have experienced by now, meditation is not

hard. But in case it has felt challenging, even though you've been practicing as instructed, remember that two forces are now at work simultaneously: (1) you're solidifying a new habit of meditating with ease, and (2) you're breaking the old habit of *not* meditating. It's breaking the sometimes decades-long habit of not meditating that can create a drag on meditation, like a headwind does on an airplane.

On your weaker days, when you may feel like throwing in the towel, don't curse meditation for being hard (that's a classic amateur mistake). Instead, *view the challenge you feel as a sign of progress.* It's a withdrawal symptom—and it's a powerful indicator that your new habit is being formed. You're moving forward down the runway, picking up speed, about to achieve liftoff! The faster you go, the more wind resistance you'll feel, as that old habit of not meditating begins fighting, clawing, and confusing your mind in countless failed attempts to slow you down and retain control over you. But because both starting the new habit and breaking the old one are happening simultaneously, meditation is going to get the blame. It always does! Or, worse, your mind gets blamed. Or the anecdotal evidence found in this book will get blamed. Or I'll get blamed. Or sometimes all four. The important thing to remember is that, no matter what happens, if you're sitting for your daily practice, you're making progress by demolishing the weak habit of not meditating.

Once you break through to the other side and achieve liftoff, meditation will feel like the easiest thing ever. But the truth is, it didn't all of a sudden get easier. *It was this easy the entire time.* The reason it begins to feel easier after ninety days is because you're no longer having to grapple with the withdrawal symptoms of not meditating.

Ninety Days to Bliss More

It bears repeating: the magic number for breaking the habit of not meditating is ninety. I want you to commit to meditating in the E.A.S.Y. way for at least ninety days straight, or three months. After around ninety days in a row, you'll be like the Cessna once it accelerates to ninety miles an hour. You'll have that "wheels up" feeling as you effortlessly achieve liftoff—meaning you'll reach a point where most of your meditations will feel mostly blissful, and you'll no longer have to spend time and energy actively planning each meditation. It'll become something you instinctively prioritize in your day, along with brushing your teeth and showering.

If you're constantly hitting the brakes, skipping days, and slowing down, you will feel as though you're expending *a lot* of energy without ever reaching that flow state that every meditator seeks inside and outside of the practice. The cutoff is ninety. Not eighty-five, not sixty-two, not every other day for ninety days. It's ninety days in a row. If you haven't already started, begin with your first meditation today. Ten minutes will do. And commit to doing at least one meditation a day, but no more than two, for ninety straight days in order to achieve liftoff. After ninety days, set a new ninety-day goal, and continue taking it in ninety-day blocks until you feel the bliss begin to stabilize more and more.

MAINTAINING CONSISTENCY IN MEDITATION

Here are some suggestions for maintaining consistency in your daily meditation practice:

Mark your calendar. Use your smartphone (or your computer, your diary, or whatever other tool you prefer) to make a daily appointment for meditation. (The advantage to using a device like a phone is that you can set notifications for the reminders to repeat daily.) Make appointments for each of the next seven days and put reminders in your phone, in your computer, on your dashboard, on your refrigerator, or wherever you stand the best chance of actually seeing the reminder.

Commit to one week. If the thought of ninety days makes you anxious, forget about the marathon and just get through this next mile. Take it one week at a time, and take that week one day at a time. Practice one meditation, then plan for tomorrow's.

Create a rewards system. After you are consistent for seven days straight, do something nice for yourself. Get together with a good friend for a nice meal, splurge on fresh flowers at the farmer's market, or get those running shoes or cozy slippers you've been eyeing—whatever works for you as a reward for your unbroken commitment.

Fine yourself for skipping. For the tough-love types, figure out how much it would be worth it for you to *not* miss meditations. In other words, if you had to pay this amount each time you skipped, you simply wouldn't skip. Ten dollars may not do it, but $50 might. Then treat missing meditations like getting a parking ticket and pay the price each time you miss. You can pay it to someone who agrees to hold you accountable. Or you can donate the money to charity (on top of making your exchange). Or you could drop it into a cookie jar. Either way, if you miss, you should be $50 lighter as a "penalty."

Get what you need. Restructure your environment so you'll have everything you need to be consistent in your first week: a reliable timing device, maybe a warm blanket, a comfortable place to sit (see blissmore.co for my suggestions on clocks and blankets). If you meditate in your car, keep a small pillow for your lower back or a blanket in your trunk. If you are going on vacation with your family, search the destination for potential meditation spots such as local hotels and churches so you have ideas of places to retreat to for quiet time. When it comes to consistency, nothing beats a little preparation.

Hang out with role models. Spend more time with people who model the habits you want to mirror. Start a *Bliss More* book and practice club, and start meditating with friends. Or join local group meditations. Or use social media to organize weekly group meditations in your area. However you do it, begin building a community of meditators around you.

Track your results. It's not necessary to interpret or analyze what you think about in meditation at this point. But it may be helpful to start a meditation journal and track how you feel after each practice. Use a simple guideline of "better, same, or worse" compared to how you felt before you meditated and jot it down, along with any epiphanies you had in your practice. Seeing how meditation lifts your mood will be powerful evidence for making it a non-negotiable priority beyond the first ninety days.

Don't be a perfectionist. Sometimes you may just have to "phone it in." That means you may be in transit, you may not have a particularly comfortable place to sit, it's a little late, or you're in a room where everyone is walking around you and you never quite feel settled. But you still do it. And doing it, as opposed to skipping it, always leaves you feeling better. Whereas skipping it always makes you feel a bit lame, because you know deep down that you could've really meditated had you planned better. Therefore, give yourself permission to *not* have perfect experiences. This includes having to get up in the middle of meditation and answer the door to sign for a package, or run to the bathroom, or put the dog outside. It's always better to deal with those situations and return to meditation than to resist them. At this point, the only bad meditation is *no* meditation.

Now let's zoom in on some finer points of meditation, including additional practices that you may desire to incorporate into your meditations.

Supplementary Practices and How to Use Them

Many people wonder whether it's okay to set intentions, say affirmations, or pray during meditation.

All of those activities are acceptable and even encouraged, as they can produce very powerful results. But they are technically still considered "activities," and as we've learned, any activities that are unnecessary for allowing the mind to roam freely will ultimately work against the E.A.S.Y. approach and diminish your overall results if employed during the meditation.

Therefore, I recommend waiting until after your meditation time is up, and using the one or two minutes you're sitting there at the end to pray, say your affirmations, or set your intentions. It's the most powerful time to engage in such actions because by then you'll have the benefit of a clearer, freshly meditated mind and a deeply rested body.

Feel free to stretch this post-meditation time out for as long as you need to get through your prayer, affirmation, or intention setting. Or, if you're feeling sleepy, you can lie down and take a nap during that time.

The one caveat is not to utilize your Settling Sound within your prayers or other supplemental practices. After a maximum of twenty minutes, you should no longer be using your Settling Sound because your meditation is technically finished. But you may transition to the other practices while sitting in the same position if you wish.

Adding Breathwork to Your Meditation

Sometimes meditators like to incorporate special breathing practices into their meditation. I have no objection to this, but breathing during meditation in any way other than how you would naturally breathe may diminish your overall results. Therefore, if you want to implement special breathing, I recommend doing so prior to beginning your meditation practice. In other words, you may sit in your meditation position, and before you start your meditation, you can begin practicing your breathwork. By the way, breathing practices can be as powerful and therapeutic as medication, so make sure that any breathwork you're doing is intentional, and that you are aware of the effects of the practice.

I also don't recommend engaging in any breathwork that wasn't prescribed to you by an expert *pranayama* (breathwork) master, kundalini master, or master yoga teacher. Most vinyasa flow yoga teachers aren't expert masters in breathwork practices, and the breathing exercises they teach in class are best suited for a movement yoga practice, not necessarily a seated meditation. So please reserve those practices for your *asana* experiences, unless specifically given permission and instructions to practice it before or after meditation by the person who taught you the technique.

YOUR FUNDAMENTALS CHECKUP

Throughout Part One, we have covered a series of instructions and refinements to your E.A.S.Y. meditation approach, but since this is a book and not a live teaching, I obviously can't address your questions as they arise. However, I have a good idea of what your lingering concerns may be going forward. Before we move into the benefits of meditation, here are some common situations that you may encounter as you acquire more experience, along with my answers.

If I don't have time to sit and meditate, can I meditate while [insert activity: running, showering, getting a massage or acupuncture]?

What's needed here is better planning and better prioritizing. You apparently have meditation in the take-out-the-trash category (something we do only if we have time). Instead, we want to put meditation in the feed-the-kids category. Make it non-negotiable—something you make time for, no matter how busy your day gets. There are 1,440 minutes in your day, and you only need ten to twenty of them to satisfy your meditation commitment.

Should I regulate my breath?

It's best to breathe normally while meditating, or you may keep your mind unnecessarily busy.

How many meditations should I do in a day?

For best results, make sure you're sitting for no more than two meditations a day, each no more than twenty minutes.

I have small children, including an infant. How do I fit meditation in between feedings and parental demands?

If you're a new parent, you may meditate in smaller increments: five minutes here, ten minutes there, in between naps and feedings. But cap it at forty minutes a day.

What do I do if I fall asleep?

There's no "if" about it. You *will* fall asleep in meditation, especially in the beginning months. And the reason is that you, like most people in our society, are sleep-deprived, and meditation will help your body pay off its sleep debt. When you start falling asleep, the way you know it's happening is you'll begin nodding off. Your head may tilt back or to the side, you may get a little wobbly, and you may have to keep catching yourself from tipping over.

Whenever you fall asleep in meditation, go with it. The way you "go with it" is to micro-adjust your body into a more horizontal position, or at the very least, rest your head back or slide down in your chair to get more comfortable. If the sleep continues to come, do not resist it. Go ahead and lie all the way down on your back and finish your meditation/nap in that position. You never want to fight sleep, and you don't have to restart your meditation. If you fall asleep during your meditation, consider that to be a part of your meditation.

That said, don't *start* your meditation lying down. Even if you feel exhausted, you should always begin your meditation while sitting relatively upright—comfortable but with your back supported. (Review the recommended positions in Chapter 1.)

If you start off meditating on your back, you're not actually meditating—you're taking a nap.

How do I handle noises?

Simply use the E.A.S.Y. approach. Treat noises—traffic, household sounds, even your own noises (a creaky knee joint, a hiccup)—in the same way you treat any other thought. Don't resist or reject noises. If you hear something that you consider to be distracting to your meditation, remain E.A.S.Y. Resist the urge to try to force the noises out of your mind. By trusting the process and keeping a passive attitude, you will eventually drift beyond the awareness of any sound you'd otherwise find distracting. Some people use earplugs to physically block out noises, but I advise against this. You don't want to become earplug-dependent in order to meditate.

Can I use an alarm?

Ideally you don't want to use a loud or jarring alarm to signal the end of the meditation, because your meditations will often feel deep and restful, and the last thing you want is to be alarmed or shocked out of that peaceful state. It doesn't take much for this to happen. Even if your alarm is a quiet gong, you'll get startled when it goes off. I recommend eyeballing the clock during meditation as many times as you have the inclination to do so. The beauty is, you'll eventually stop wondering about the time. And any inclination to check the time will get automatically overridden by your body's internal clock, which will let you know that it's only been a few minutes, and then you get lost in another thought without ever having to peek.

Is it okay to jot down good ideas I have while meditating so I don't forget them?

It's best not to. The point of meditation is to stay relaxed. Writing in the middle of meditation *excites* the mind and body. If it's a truly important thought or idea, you'll most likely remember it after you complete your meditation.

If I keep overmeditating, should I use an alarm?

Overmeditating will happen naturally from time to time. You don't need an alarm unless you have something important to do immediately after the meditation. Then, yes, you may use an alarm, but make sure it's a soft alarm (don't worry, you'll hear it), and set it for twenty-five minutes as a cushion; the hope is that you'll come out naturally.

How best should I enter and exit meditation?

Ideally, you want to start with an easy transition into the meditation, and a gradual transition out of meditation. That means you don't want to just plop down and start thinking your Settling Sound right away. You want to ease into it, after first relaxing your physical body. And at the end of the meditation, for best results, you want to ease out of the practice. If you come out of the meditation too abruptly, you may become a little grumpy, or edgy, or disoriented. Always give yourself a minute or two before you open your eyes for good at the end of the meditation.

This applies to ten-minute meditations, too. Always exit meditation gradually as opposed to abruptly.

You've now received all of the fundamentals for succeeding in meditation without really trying. Next we're going to delve into the real-world benefits, so you know without a doubt that your meditation is indeed working—in spite of the sometimes weird, bizarre, or strange emotions you may experience in your meditation.

Part Two

WHY WE MEDITATE
The Benefits

7

WHY IT WORKS

Did meditation really help the Seattle Seahawks—the statistical underdogs in Super Bowl XLVIII—demolish the Denver Broncos 43 to 8? Some people certainly thought so.

Weeks after the carnage in MetLife Stadium, there was Seattle quarterback Russell Wilson, photographed in lotus pose with his thumbs and index fingers together (dressed in his uniform) for a *Psychology Today* article titled "How Meditation Won the Super Bowl." The writer cited the influence of "mindfulness practices," encouraged for years by Seahawks coach Pete Carroll, as the secret ingredient behind the Seahawks' decisive victory.

This sent the meditation community into a frenzy, with meditation teachers everywhere "sharing" the article all over social media, often with an "I told you so." The article actually only mentions that the players were "encouraged" to meditate by their coach. Apparently a sports psychologist was brought in to teach them some "mindfulness techniques"—which, if you read between the lines, could mean anything. It was a fun headline for us in the meditation community to see, but to surmise that meditation was the true MVP of the 2013 world football championship is a stretch. In its exaggeration, the article brings to mind infomercial claims that a certain training regimen or protein powder will result in amazing six-pack abs "in just twenty-one days!" Or that if you "just ask your doctor for a prescription," a pharmaceutical will finally cure your blues or relieve your irritable bowel syndrome or revive your libido.

The subject of meditation claims in pop culture, as well as in academic and scientific publications, leads to a larger issue that I feel needs to be addressed as we now delve into the many benefits of meditation: how the rosy conclusions of meditation studies compare with the real-world experiences of average Joes and Janes—the folks who, like you and me, are out there meditating on park benches, in bedrooms, and in broom closets.

Over my years of personally training and supporting thousands of individuals to meditate, and tracking their experiences, I have heard some quite remarkable stories of how normal people have benefited from their practice. But full disclosure: meditation or not, we're all a work in progress.

For instance, I personally know meditators who still chain-smoke or are sugar addicts. I know meditators who still grapple with anger management issues, who have relapsed into substance abuse, who are train wrecks in relationships. You name the issue, and I'll bet you there is a dedicated daily meditator who is experiencing it on some level right now.

The problem is that when we come across clickbait articles highlighting exaggerated claims around meditation—especially without mentioning the fine print in the study being reported—the expectation is that *your* meditation practice will be a panacea that will instantly transform you into an overly grateful, peace-and-love pacifist health nut, with Super Bowl strength and an Einstein brain.

"Meditation Weakened Chocolate Cravings Among People with a Self-Described Sweet Tooth!" If you came across a headline such as that one (it's real), coupled with a stock photo of an attractive woman meditating in a whitewashed room with a delicious piece of chocolate placed on a plate in front of her, you would probably think that meditation is indeed a miracle activity. Who among us can resist chocolate? Apparently those of us who meditate can.

If anyone bothered to read the article—or, better yet, the original study it describes, conducted by psychologists at Canada's McGill University—they'll see how researchers recruited 196 participants to either undergo "meditation training" or be part of a group that received no training. Those who were trained were divided into four groups and taught various "mindfulness meditation techniques"—which is like saying they cooked using various "cooking techniques." Then they were directed to practice their technique whenever a chocolate craving arose over the next two weeks, while members of the fifth group were told to distract themselves to fend off cravings. Two weeks later, participants were given a piece of chocolate to unwrap and touch for one minute; afterward the chocolate was snatched away, and they rated how much they craved the candy.

The headline implied that meditators were somehow able to resist chocolate more than the non-meditators, but the study itself doesn't address whether meditation techniques can change the cravings we experience beyond two weeks. The researchers state that more investigation is needed on the long-term ability of meditation to combat cravings and that "real changes" may require *thousands* of hours of practice!

This is but one story among many where the benefits of meditation—including those documented in a legitimate scientific study—get completely hyped up and only the juicy bits make the news. When meditation studies make popular headlines, I guarantee that you are only reading a fraction of a fraction of the story—and even most authors of such studies would agree that not all their results are being reported accurately and interpreted properly for the layperson.

What Meditation Really Does

I had been meditating for around three years when I started dating a woman who, shortly after we met, became a committed daily meditator. Our relationship started off great—we felt a lot of unity, and we were extremely passionate. However, several months in, she and I began bickering and nitpicking at one another's words and actions. Our fights became more and more frequent as the months progressed and our relationship declined.

One night at her apartment, she wanted to discuss an argument we had had earlier in the day. It was late and all I wanted to do was sleep so I could get up early for an appointment, but it was clear she wasn't going to let it go. Exasperated, I decided to head back to my place rather than continue to argue. Her response was to block the door. In full stress mode, heart racing, I darted out around her and into the alley. She ran after me, chasing me down the block. I don't even know why we were running, except to say we were both in fight-or-flight mode. I reached my car, got in, and sped off, certain that the relationship was finished. But a few days later, we made up and continued seeing each other for another six months (and several more rounds of late-night arguing).

Now, if you come across a headline saying, "Study Suggests Meditation Improves Relationships and Reduces Co-Dependency" (and I have seen reports just like that), you may think that surely after three years of daily practice, a person like me—a future meditation teacher, with a meditating girlfriend, no less—should have a perfectly functional relationship. On the contrary, we were the flipside of that study . . . the question no study asks is "What would've happened had we not been meditators?"

We will never know how much more turbulent our relationship might have been had we not been meditating. Perhaps a late-night argument might've turned violent. Or we might have remained in the dysfunctional relationship for three more years instead of only six months. We might have gotten married, thinking it would solve our problems!

My point is this: rather than have you look to meditation studies, I encourage consistent meditators of all traditions and experience levels to compare where they are today—mentally, emotionally, physically, and spiritually—with where they were five years ago (or ninety days ago), and you will likely see stark differences in just about every area of your life. Forget the headline hype and ask yourself the following: Are you less dramatic? More compassionate? Do you have less anger? Are you less of a train wreck in relationships? These are the real-world ways you should be accurately measuring progress in meditation.

In my work with thousands of meditators all over the world, I have never met a person who devolved into a worse version of themselves after they began to meditate. Even for people who are in a dramatic situation—like my former relationship— meditation seems to help with awareness of the drama, which is the first step toward deescalating it.

The reason I'm telling you this now is that I don't want you finishing this book thinking that meditation is a magic bullet that will solve all of your deeply rooted personal and professional problems and, in the process, transform you into a saint. It's not. And you definitely aren't on a track to sainthood! While some of the studies on meditation are completely legitimate, with realistic conclusions, results can still vary widely from person to person depending on who was being studied, what style they practiced, how they were taught, how long they had been meditating prior to being studied, and, most important, what kind of environment they were in at the time they were studied. These variables will rarely, if ever, match your own direct experiences.

The White Coat Phenomenon—and What It Led To

The "white coat phenomenon" occurs when a patient's blood pressure is measurably higher when being checked by a physician or other clinician in a medical setting, versus when self-measured at home. The spike in blood pressure has been attributed to the increase in anxiety from hearing the potentially negative results from an authority figure. When a patient is measuring his own blood pressure at home, he often records better results due to lowered anxiety levels from having no authority figures evaluating, examining, or observing him.

Although the white coat phenomenon has been mainly cited in reference to blood pressure (because it's easy to measure independent of a doctor), it has not been seen as a hindrance to studying meditation—but perhaps it should be. I find that meditation can be as intimate and personal as bathing, sleeping, or even self-pleasuring. Imagine how stressed you might be if an "outsider"—like a researcher in a lab coat—was observing and judging your performance as you engaged in any of those activities! I'm not a scientist, and I'm not suggesting that *all* of the results of meditation studies are tainted. In spite of their glaring limitations, meditation studies have still shown remarkable results.

Evidently, the brains and bodies of meditators are so deeply transformed that even under the harshest of lab conditions this ancient practice is still quite resilient. Consider that meditating in a hard-backed chair with distractions like electrodes, cold air-conditioning, fluorescent lighting, and someone directing your meditation—"Focus on this. Think of that. Breathe this way"—is the exact opposite of the E.A.S.Y. approach. If you've been practicing as instructed, then you can only imagine how much more profound the results would be if you are meditating in a natural, comfortable environment, alone, and with complete permission to be E.A.S.Y. with all experiences.

There aren't many studies (or, probably, any studies) that can accurately reflect what it's really like to take the initial steps outlined in Part One as you learn to meditate the E.A.S.Y. way. No study exists that measures the power of making a meaningful exchange, or what happens as you eventually meditate daily on the couch in the morning after your run, in your car at lunchtime, in your aunt's living room while the rest of the family is watching television, at a music festival behind a food truck, or in any of the other real-world settings where you will most likely be meditating. But there is one study that comes close to accurately reflecting what happens in real-world meditation.

The Discovery of the Relaxation Response

Herbert Benson was a teenager in Yonkers, New York, when his father died unexpectedly of a heart attack. This unfortunate event inspired a lifetime of curiosity in the science of stress and the mind's ability to heal the body. Benson first trained as a cardiologist and later became a professor and researcher at Harvard Medical School, where he studied blood pressure in monkeys experiencing the fight-or-flight stress response. (Benson's observations became the basis for the understanding of the white coat phenomenon when he noted that his heart disease patients had higher blood pressure readings in his office versus when they measured their own blood pressure at home.)

One day, Dr. Benson was contacted by meditators from the local Transcendental Meditation center in Cambridge. This was in the 1960s, when TM was gaining traction thanks to the growing celebrity interest in the technique, particularly after the Beatles were spotted at TM's ashram in northern India. TM had been reported to relax the nervous system and counterbalance stress, and meditators also suspected that they were lowering their blood pressure during meditation. But there were no published scientific studies backing up TM's health claims at the time, and the center in Cambridge wanted a respected medical researcher like Benson to verify their claims.

From Dr. Benson's perspective, the reason no major medical school or research institution had studied the effects of meditation before was because, in the West, meditation wasn't viewed as a legitimate healing modality for the body, and therefore it didn't merit research, as that would be an obvious waste of time—after all, the mind and body behave separately, or so the medical community thought. He turned down the center's request to study their work. But the meditators were convinced that something profound was indeed happening and remained persistent. Dr. Benson, whom I interviewed while researching this book, told me he turned them down a second time and then a third. The meditators finally got through to him with the argument "Why are you fooling around with monkeys to study blood pressure when you can study us?"

As Dr. Benson learned more about the TM technique, his resistance began to soften. What if the link between the mind and body could be proven through measuring the effects of meditation? Furthermore, out of all the approaches to meditation, he noted that the teaching and practicing of TM had certain qualities that would make it ideal for scientific study—the uniformity of the teaching style, the initiation practices, and the practice length would give him ways to control his experiments. He also appreciated the possible link between meditation and blood pressure levels, the very thing that had led him to medical research in the first place.

He relented and agreed to study a volunteer group of Transcendental Meditation practitioners (with an average of two to three years' experience, and from all walks of life) in his lab, but only after regular hours. Though he was the target of intense ridicule from his colleagues, Dr. Benson invited the TMers into the Thorndike Laboratory at Harvard Medical School (coincidentally, the same lab where, forty years earlier, Harvard physiologist Dr. Walter Cannon mapped out the physiological changes that occur during the stress response and named the reaction "fight-or-flight") and began measuring the effects of meditation on as many aspects of human physiology as he could think of.

He tested for oxygen consumption (which is the primary indicator of rest), blood lactate (an indicator of anxiety), heart rate, respiration, eye movement, blood pressure, alpha waves (the brain waves responsible for relaxation), and even fluctuations in rectal temperature (rectal temperature decreases with hibernation, and Dr. Benson wanted to examine whether the meditator was sleeping, hibernating, or something else). Over subsequent studies, he poked and prodded the meditators, recorded them, asked them questions in the middle of their meditation, manipulated the time, issued placebo mantras, and threw in any other variation he could think of.

What Dr. Benson discovered both surprised and scared him. Meditators weren't sleeping, hibernating, or fully awake. They were experiencing a previously undocumented physiological state that had never before been seen in a laboratory with "regular" people who happened to meditate. According to his data, meditation was not just restful but deeply restful—even more restful than sleep when the two experiences are compared minute for minute. Dr. Benson had uncovered a fourth state of consciousness, one that was of the same level of significance as waking, dreaming, and sleeping. Twenty minutes of TM, he observed, put the body into a state of rest that was equivalent to an hour of deep sleep. Dr. Benson also noted significant decreases in the heart rate, oxygen consumption, respiratory rate, and blood pressure of his meditating subjects—indicating that Transcendental Meditation induced a physiological state different from any other experience. Thanks to the persistence of the meditators combined with his passion for researching stress, Dr. Benson stumbled upon a nearly perfect, endogenous (meaning "produced within the body") solution to the stress response—one proving his theory that the mind does have an influence over the body. He was scared because he knew that announcing the results of his research was going to upset many of his more traditional colleagues who staunchly believed that the mind and body behaved independently of each other.

While he was shaving one morning, the name for his radical discovery occurred to him: the *relaxation response.* The phrase was parallel to Dr. Cannon's "stress response," but the state itself had the exact opposite effect on the nervous system. Instead of inducing high blood pressure, the relaxation response activated the parasympathetic nervous system, which lowered blood pressure in those meditators with high blood pressure and had a neutral effect in the rest. Instead of thickening the blood, as happened with the fight-or-flight stress response, meditation worked as a natural blood thinner. Instead of increasing the heart and respiratory rates, meditation lowered them, suggesting a profoundly more restful state.

Being a scientist, Dr. Benson naturally began to wonder: if the stress response could be triggered by a variety of experiences, shouldn't the same apply to the relaxation response? He began to dissect the TM technique in search of the active ingredients. He was curious if it was the mantra, the body position, the passive attitude, or the length of time that was most responsible for the dramatic state of relaxation that occurs within the body. He began experimenting with sounds other than the traditional TM mantras, and dozens of experiments later, Dr. Benson discovered that indeed it wasn't just TM that could produce the relaxation response.

If the meditator sat comfortably, maintained a similarly passive attitude during meditation, and used a point of focus such as a mantra, a Settling Sound, a prayer, or an affirmation, within a twenty-minute time span this deeply restful response could be easily and reliably replicated. His 1975 bestseller, *The Relaxation Response,* which distilled his suggested technique, sold more than four million copies, is still in print, and solidified Dr. Benson's standing as a highly regarded figure in mind-body research, of which he was a pioneer.

Dr. Benson's initial skeptical study turned into decades of devoted research on the relaxation response and eventually became the foundation for today's suggestion (from a variety of health experts) that daily meditation can significantly reduce your chances of falling victim to the most prevalent Western killers: heart disease, cancer, and transportation accidents. It can reduce your reliance on pharmaceutical medication as well. Also, when a daily meditator has less stress and more rest, she develops a stronger immune system, suffers less from insomnia, sees an increase in fertility, and experiences less depression.

Dr. Benson's relaxation response describes the necessary conditions for inducing the most desirable outcome of meditation—relaxing the parasympathetic nervous system, which offsets the destructive effects of stress on sleep, digestion, reproduction, and immunity. The relaxation response is both a specific technique and a description of the state of the nervous system under the influence of similar approaches that use a passive attitude, a "soothing, mellifluous sound," and a comfortable seat. This is essentially the E.A.S.Y. approach to meditating that you have been learning about and, I hope, using. But the most attractive benefit is that this passive approach, free of physical and mental control or manipulation, is enjoyable to practice.

A major difference between Dr. Benson's approach and the one I describe here, however, is his specific use of the word "focus" in his instructions. As you know by now, being directed to focus makes meditation practice less enjoyable—and consequently harder. (Because Dr. Benson wasn't trained as a meditation teacher, he probably didn't realize that TM teachers avoid using the word "focus" because it doesn't fit with maintaining a passive attitude.)

Like the relaxation response, the E.A.S.Y. meditation approach is intended to create a state of restful mental awareness, which in turn relaxes your nervous system. Because it follows Dr. Benson's template (based on the TM technique), the process can produce a similar effect in the body of the meditator that will lead to enhanced rest. (This is based solely on anecdotal evidence, as there have been no official studies conducted on the E.A.S.Y. approach. But the majority of my students, most of whom learned with me in person, have reported achieving a significantly better quality of rest while sleeping at night.)

Anytime our body gets an opportunity to rest profoundly and deeply, as has been shown by Dr. Benson to occur during most passive approaches to meditation, it can release stress. In other words, high-quality rest leads to the release of stress, or "de-stressing," as it is sometimes referred to. (If you'd like, think of it this way: If stress is a cockroach, then meditation is like a can of Raid. You just have to use it.)

Indeed, one of the fastest-acting benefits I've witnessed in my students who adhere to the E.A.S.Y. approach to meditation is improved sleep. Let's look at this benefit more closely, since improved rest has a cascade of immediate, real-world effects on well-being—both mental (clearer thinking, more happiness, less stress) and physical (less sickness, less stress).

8

THE SLEEP EFFECT

In the West, we are by and large a functionally sleep-deprived society—and sleep deprivation severely and directly affects our physical and mental health. When we're short on sleep, we can't remember things, nor can we concentrate, react quickly, or communicate properly. Our cardiovascular health takes a hit, along with our digestive system, fertility, weight, and so much more. The inability to sleep can even kill—consider the astonishing number of accidents, more than 100,000 a year, caused by drivers who fall asleep at the wheel.

A study conducted by the AAA Foundation for Traffic Safety compared sleepy drivers with legally intoxicated drivers, and found that drunks can drive circles around sleep-deprived drivers in driving tests. The study also noted that driving while sleepy is the number one cause of traffic accidents, most of which occur between 2:00 a.m. and 3:00 a.m., the time of night when we're most tired. Another study by researchers in Australia showed that missing a night's sleep produced an impairment that is worse than being legally drunk.

Sleep deprivation accumulates gradually over time. A missed hour. An all-nighter. A red-eye flight. The baby's up crying three nights in a row. Up late watching a movie. Tossing and turning thinking about a conversation that didn't go well earlier that day. Not to mention all the partying and all-nighters in college. It adds up.

There's a thought experiment often explained in psychology classes that demonstrates the subtle but devastating effect of sleep deprivation on our minds and bodies—a story I frequently share in my trainings. When discussing stress management, a professor might hold up a glass of water and ask the class, "How heavy is this?" Answers usually range from eight to twenty ounces. The professor will go on to explain that while the guesses may be on target, for a true determination of heaviness, the absolute weight is not as important as the *length of time* you hold the glass.

Think of it this way: if you hold a glass for a minute, even if it's twenty ounces, it feels light. But if you hold it for an hour, even if it weighs just eight ounces, it'll feel so heavy that you'll most likely have an ache in your arm. And if you have to hold it all day, you'll probably require medical attention.

In each case the glass of water could be the same weight, but the longer you hold it, the more taxing it is on your mind and body. And that's the effect that long-term stress has on our bodies. If we keep going all the time—doing, doing, doing—with little to no rest, then sooner or later, as the small burdens of life accumulate and become increasingly heavier, our ability to function optimally will be compromised by something seemingly insignificant.

In order to be more productive, we must take frequent periods of rest. Rest has always been the basis for relieving the debilitating effects of stress, achieving balance, and accessing our full potential.

GETTING SLEEPY

My first impression of Otto was that he could be an actual vampire.

I was standing outside of St. Paul's Cathedral in the Wicker Park area of Chicago when a young man wearing a black trench coat, baggy black pants, and black army boots strolled up to me and asked if this was where the meditation talk was being held. His pale, round face and scraggly blond facial hair were hidden behind his dark oval sunglasses and a black cap pulled low over his brow. His voice was scratchy, as if he'd spent a significant amount of time smoking or yelling.

Turns out it was both. Otto was a chain-smoking radio disc jockey by night and a Cracker Jack and cotton candy salesman at Wrigley Field by day. He didn't mind the back-to-back schedule, he once told me, because he wasn't a sleeper. Apparently he was only sleeping an average of ten hours a *week,* and the day I met him he had been awake for seventy-two hours.

Of course he wanted to sleep, and tried to, but he couldn't.

He would lie down in bed and close his eyes, but his sleep was light at best, and it would inevitably not last beyond an hour or two. He had first noticed the quality of his sleep beginning to diminish about eleven years before, when he moved out of his parents' home—although he said it hadn't been great before then, either.

While some define insomnia as four hours of sleep a night or less, Otto would consider four hours to be a luxury. In all of his years of battling insomnia, he had discovered one hack: for some reason, he could sleep on a city bus. So he purposely sought out jobs that required him to take long bus rides, where he could stay asleep until the last stop, at which point he would be awakened by the driver.

By the time we met, Otto was beyond desperation. He'd read that a lack of sleep could cause brain damage and that sleep deprivation was potentially more destructive to the brain than being hooked on crack. He'd also read that going four or five days without sleep would make someone become legally insane, and going more than eleven days without sleep could kill you. (Otto claimed to have done both numerous times. He told me that he'd gone an entire month where the only sleep he got was during his fifteen-minute bus rides to and from work.)

The only time Otto recalled being able to get a good night's sleep was when he was in a romantic relationship, and only when it was going well. Unfortunately, in his case this meant his good sleep usually didn't last long, and resulted in more sleepless nights processing the failure of his dating life.

Otto was convinced that meditating would have a "nocebo" effect—zero impact on him—that it would fail, just like everything else he'd tried, including exercise, valerian root, Ambien, Xanax, and prodigious drinking. He had even tried to teach himself "image streaming," stream-of-consciousness daydreaming that purportedly can replace REM sleep. (I've found insomniacs to be particularly well-versed in crackpot "sleep hack" experiments prior to exploring meditation.)

As it turned out, Otto had experimented off and on with meditation before he came to my talk. The previous year, he'd toured across the American South on Greyhound buses, making and playing experimental music in cafés and hole-in-the-wall bars. Before leaving on his trip, he'd found a book on meditation at a used-book store, and gave the techniques a try. To his surprise, they worked like a charm. But he still wasn't sure if it was solely the meditation. After all, he was riding buses. Two weeks in, his nocebo kicked in as his progress began to wane. He stopped meditating, convinced that it was indeed the bus and not the meditation that was responsible for his sleep.

Otto later admitted that he probably gave up on meditation too early, because he didn't know any better and figured he was meditating incorrectly. Otherwise, he said, he would have persisted. Even so, he decided that his experience from the meditation book was substantial enough to merit further exploration, because when a stranger (one of my students) back in Chicago saw Otto reading his meditation book on the train one day, he gave him my phone number.

The first night I met Otto, he introduced himself and then sat alone in the empty basement room waiting for others to arrive. He never removed his sunglasses during the entire session. Normally I can glance around the room and tell who's into my talk and who's not based on their eye contact. I had no idea with Otto. To my surprise, he came up to me afterward and expressed genuine interest in joining the training, which began the next day. I happily agreed to accept him as a student. For his exchange, he presented me with $200 in ones and fives that he'd collected selling concessions at Cubs games over the past week. And later I received an email alerting me that "captain-fuckhead" (Otto's PayPal handle) had sent me an additional $200.

Despite his eccentricities (or perhaps because of them), Otto turned out to be a model student. He paid close attention during the instruction, challenged me on the academic studies that I quoted to explain the inner workings of meditation, asked relevant questions, and did his home practices. As I expected, he reported positive results once he began meditating on his own. Here's an excerpt from a check-in email exchange between Otto and me a few years after we met, when he recalled his first day after learning how to meditate:

> When you gave me my [Settling Sound] and I started repeating it, I immediately felt a restful feeling rolling over the muscles in my face. Just from that, I felt extremely rested and energized for the rest of the day, until I sat down at a restaurant to eat, and then it dissipated.

I walked home and slept for about 15 hours, waking up only to feed my cat. Then I woke up and went to work, and came home, and again, slept for 15 hours, and went to work. When I didn't work, I slept for three days straight. Most of my summer was like that, for about three months. I get a bit misty now thinking about it. The summer of 2011, I slept through most of it, and it brings me joy to think about it. Scientists have said that you can't catch up on lost sleep, but I don't believe them.

I've kept in touch with Otto over the years, and he has a noticeable meditator's glow, common with longer-term meditators. He reports sleeping more regularly, and whenever he comes back to audit one of my trainings, he seems more open, attentive, warm, and compassionate. Also, whenever I see him now, he removes his sunglasses.

Otto still considers himself to be a "recovering insomniac." Yet the amount of rest he gets these days from sleep is significant. Though he still has the occasional sleepless night, it's usually because he's excited from working on a new experimental music project that he can't get off his mind.

In my experience, meditation can prompt you to fall asleep. In fact, it's not unusual to fall asleep *a lot* in the early days of meditation. Night owls may find themselves passing out earlier in the evening, and early birds may find themselves sleeping later than usual. Whenever it happens, go with it! Once you pay off more of your sleep debt, you'll enjoy a much higher quality of rest both in sleep and meditation.

Reports from the Field: The End of Insomnia

I was desperate to reunite with an old friend, sleep. For most of my life, I usually didn't fall asleep until 1:00 or 2:00 a.m. and consequently have never been a morning person. But over the past year it has become increasingly worse: 1:00 or 2:00 a.m. became 3:00 or 4:00, sometimes 5:00, and waking up before 10:00 a.m. became impossible. I had no idea how to fix it. I would have so many thoughts swirling around in my mind at night and couldn't turn them off. I couldn't even slow them down. It was torture to feel physically exhausted every night but not be able to slip into unconsciousness. Meditation changed all that. Even after just two days of meditating, I was asleep by 11:00 p.m. and awake by 7:30 a.m. Two years after starting, I'm in bed no later than midnight and sleep well through the night, waking up early for work without an alarm clock or an attitude. This approach to meditation truly changed my life.

—Amber

For the first time ever, I fell asleep at the end of my afternoon meditation today. It may have been one of the most magical experiences I've ever had. The sun was just coming across the window, I felt the heat on my arm, and the next thing I knew it was one hour later. Anyone who knows me knows I have never been an easy sleeper, and certainly not

in a chair, for heaven's sake. I can barely sleep in a bed. Un-
real!

—*Vicki*

The sleep effect is closely related to the body's release of
stress, also known as the de-stressing process. The higher the
quality of rest, the better the chances that our body can reestab-
lish balance through daily doses of meditation and better sleep.
But the stress-release phenomenon comes with its own often
unanticipated array of strange sensations and weird side effects.
And as you'll see in the next chapter, these experiences—bizarre
as they may seem—are not only beneficial but symptomatic of
correct practice.

9

STRESS LESS (BLISS MORE)

Let me ask you a few questions. (Hold your "Oh yeah! That explains it!" reaction till you get to the end of this list.)

- Have you had any strange emotions, such as crying, growing anxious, or feeling depressed, in any of your meditations? I'm specifically referring to emotions that seemed to be more or less unrelated to your current life outside of meditation.
- Have you had bizarre memories from your distant past come up in any of your meditations?
- Have you felt any weird sensations while meditating? Maybe you heard a ringing, or you smelled, tasted, or felt something that seemed to be out of place?
- Has your body been behaving strangely in meditation— you know, heating up, or shaking mildly? Has your eye

started twitching? Maybe you felt your heart begin racing
in a meditation or two? Or you felt like you stopped
breathing momentarily and had to take a big gasp of air?

If you've experienced any of those symptoms, you've had
tangible feelings of the stress release that occurs when the body
is exposed to high-quality rest environments, such as deep sleep
and meditation—though, as we'll discuss, sleep and meditation
are qualitatively different states.

We've all felt weird, bizarre, and strange emotions and sensations occur over the course of the night while sleeping (and
dreaming). Because both meditation *and* sleep induce rest, it's
possible to have the same kinds of sensations in both experiences. In other words, whenever you feel strange sensations in
meditation, it's not because you're doing something wrong, or
because evil spirits are invading your body. Instead, it's because
your body is resting at a profoundly deep level, and as a result, it
is mimicking the sensations of sleep—*except you may not be falling
asleep*. You're meditating. And as Dr. Benson noted in his extensive research, while meditating and sleeping are both restful
states, physiologically they are entirely distinct.

Mental rest acquired through meditation leads to deep physical rest. And physical rest leads to rehabilitation in the body. In
other words, the more rested your body becomes in meditation
(or during sleep), the more stress it can release. There is no meditation research I'm aware of that has scientifically verified the
phenomenon of how meditation helps to release stress (though
there's also no science I'm aware of that *negates* the claim). Re-

gardless, I'm going to show you how to do your own research on whether or not meditation triggers stress release—based solely on your personal experiences. If you've been meditating as instructed and you've practiced at least a dozen times, you should now be able to identify the symptoms that confirm stress release. Here are some counterintuitive yet common symptoms that your body is releasing stress during meditation:

- Weird sensations, feelings, or memories
- Strange sounds, visuals, or smells
- Heart racing
- The body heating up or cooling down
- Becoming itchy
- Incessant coughing or burping
- Sweaty palms or feet
- Tearing up or crying
- Dizziness
- A feeling of heaviness
- Feelings of anxiety or depression
- Dark or negative thoughts
- Restlessness
- Mild to extreme boredom
- Thoughts racing through the mind
- Bad dreams

As you'll also experience, the stress dissolution process will sometimes lead to seemingly random spikes in physical and mental activity during portions of a twenty-minute meditation, or throughout the entire meditation.

The culprit is not your mischievous mind, as amateur meditators often assume. The true cause behind a rocky meditation is a body that is innocently (yet efficiently) purging old stress. What happens when you soak in the bathtub after a long hot day of gardening? Your body gets clean and the water gets kind of dirty. With meditation, the rest is cleansing the body, and this can sometimes dirty the mental and physical experiences, leading to a spike in activity. This is one of the reasons your mind may not feel particularly settled in some meditations, despite the fact that you're practicing the E.A.S.Y. approach as instructed. So remember, weird sensations and surprising or strange emotions are *common* symptoms of your body rehabilitating itself. In short, nothing "bad" is happening. When de-stressing occurs again and you happen to notice it in meditation, maintain your carefree attitude, and passively return to your Settling Sound to remain engaged in the purification process.

FLEEING OVER THE RAINBOW: HIDDEN STRESS TRIGGERS

Whenever we can achieve deep rest through meditation or sleep, we also place our body into a position where it will neutralize the triggers associated with past stress experiences, or memories. There are two broad categories of memories that we tend to hang on to and store in our bodies: happy memories, which are tied to situations we enjoyed and successfully adapted to; and stress-related memories, linked to circumstances that we mal-adapted or overreacted to—situations that triggered our stress response defense mechanism.

When I taught yoga in the early 2000s, I loved choosing just the right songs for each portion of my class. One night I discovered the version of "Over the Rainbow" performed by the late Hawaiian musician Israel "Iz" Ka'ano'i Kamakawiwo'ole. I thought it would be perfect to use as we transitioned from the intense and sweaty standing sequences into the deep floor stretches, indicating that the cooling-down period had begun.

The next evening, when I played it, the most bizarre and un-expected thing happened. A woman who was a regular in my classes jumped up as if she'd seen a ghost, grabbed all of her belongings, and fled from the room, knocking over people's props as she darted out. Needless to say, that wasn't the reaction I'd been imagining when I added this sweet, soothing song to my playlist!

I didn't see her in class for about three weeks. Then one day she returned. Before class began she approached me with an apologetic look on her face. "I'm so sorry for leaving so abruptly," she said.

"Yeah, what was that all about?" I asked.

"Well, do you remember you played that song, 'Over the Rainbow'?"

I nodded.

"Earlier that day, my husband of four years told me that he was leaving me for another woman, and 'Over the Rainbow' was our wedding song. So as soon as I heard it come on . . . I don't know what came over me, but I just had to get out of there as quickly as possible. Please don't play that song again today."

What I found interesting about her experience was that this was a smart woman. She was a lawyer, and like many serious yogis, she was very well-read spiritually. She knew her yogic and Eastern philosophy. And yet when she heard the opening chords of a sweet little song about rainbows, lullabies, and bluebirds, it became impossible for her to stay in the room because it triggered a physical reaction to danger. To her body, she was under attack, and the song was the attacker. But it wasn't the song that was the source of the reaction. The *source* was the stress reaction she had had earlier that morning, when she was faced with a stark change of expectation involving her marriage. The song was the trigger. Truthfully, it could have been anything—a scent, a color, the weather—that reminded her of her broken marriage, and the reaction likely would have been the same.

The Anatomy of the Stress Response

To better understand the impact of meditation on stress release, let's look at how the fight-or-flight reaction works. You're driving while texting, or while sleepy, or while daydreaming, and you're in stop-and-go traffic. A moment later, you glance up and realize that the car in front of you has stopped, so you quickly slam on your brakes in order to avoid impact. Either you stop breathing momentarily or you begin hyperventilating, and you feel your heart pounding. You've never been more alert. The potential collision gave rise to a stressful wave of fear. "I almost hit that person!" you think. "Thank God I was able to brake in time." That's what it feels like to experience the stress reaction.

Whenever we experience a surge of distress such as fear, sadness, or anger, our bodies and brains react quickly and in tandem in order to help us escape some potentially life-threatening danger—like a car accident or an unexpected run-in with a hungry tiger or angry silverback gorilla. To aid in the accompanying survival reaction, we have been genetically engineered to produce powerful—yet toxic—chemicals that supply us with superhuman strength and speed, which increase our odds of survival (though they may temporarily disrupt our normal biological needs, such as sleeping or eating—who wants to stop for lunch when you're about to *be* lunch?).

We are all the evolutionary descendants of the humans who reacted the quickest to threats and danger throughout hundreds of thousands of years of hunting and gathering in the wild. The humans who tried to reason with the tiger or silverback gorilla didn't live long enough to have offspring. Therefore, the stress reaction gene is hardwired into each of *us,* and it comes in very handy when we're under the threat of danger. But when the perceived attacker is just a traffic jam, the body doesn't distinguish between the line of cars ahead making us late for work and a potential silverback gorilla attack. It treats all such distressful emotions the same way—fear, sadness, anger, even boredom. In other words, your mind says, *Get me out of here, now!* And your body responds accordingly.

You may be quite familiar with that aspect of the fight-or-flight reaction, but associated memories, or stress triggers, can feel just as threatening as a snarling wild animal. Stress triggers are stored deep in the body's memory bank as lifelong reminders of all the sensations that were present during a traumatic episode—again, a worthwhile survival feature. Imagine that you somehow got attacked by a silverback gorilla while waiting in line at the post office, and lived to tell the tale. Chances are that for the rest of your life, your body would preemptively warn you about the high potential of a deadly gorilla attack every time you even thought about going to a post office. For you, the entire post office experience—mail, stamps, envelopes, letter carriers, the deep blue and red colors, the phrase "Priority Mail," long lines, white mail trucks, or anything else having to do with the postal service—will trigger a feeling of danger that will be very difficult to turn off once it begins.

In the case of my yoga student, she grew sad and/or angry when her husband told her he was leaving her. Physiologically, her body registered these emotions as a threat—her way of life was about to change, after all—and so anything that she perceived as linked to her attacker (her husband) might trigger a similar "we're under attack" response in her body. These "threats" could include things like his cologne, his voice, his image in photographs, favorite foods and vacation spots, and of course the song that was played at their wedding.

Under the influence of stress, previously happy or neutral memories become a trip wire for activating stress reactions, often during inopportune times and in inappropriate places. This is why if you are involved in a traumatic breakup, relationship experts recommend hiding photos and letters or any personal effects or objects that remind you of your ex while you're trying to move on. If emotions are still raw and you encounter any items or sensations reminding you of the trauma (especially when you least expect it to happen, like in a yoga class with strangers), the body will, in essence, relive the trauma—it'll automatically thrust you deep into the stress response.

Stress triggers allowed early humans to survive, and they can still help us today. But while they serve to keep us alive in the event of real danger, they can also trigger us at inopportune times, such as in traffic, at work, or at the family dinner table—even in an innocent yoga class. Left unchecked, stress triggers rob us of our ability to be happy and feel present in non-life-threatening situations.

I've had meditation students pull me to the side and admit that they rely on a stressful environment to produce their best work or to generate creativity, and that they are worried that becoming mentally calmer and more peaceful through meditation would diminish their creativity. I usually point out that what they are really referring to are demanding and high-pressure environments—not necessarily the stress response. Being truly stressed means you are experiencing a flood of toxic chemicals that allow you to run like a cheetah or fight like the Incredible Hulk—neither of which is particularly productive in the long term for work, relationships, sleep, or your health.

But there's nothing wrong with using high-pressure situations to get you out of your comfort zone and into a more creative headspace. Like many busy professionals, I've often been overscheduled and found myself thriving in demanding situations. (As the saying goes, if you need something done, give it to a busy person.) Demands are welcome. But over the long term, stress is an unnecessary distraction and impediment to productivity.

The best indicator that you are trapped in a stress response is when your reaction is out of proportion to whatever triggered it (like dashing out of a yoga class and staying away from class for almost a month, all because of a three-minute ukulele song), which is why it's also referred to as an *over*reaction or *mal*adaptation. I'm sure we can all think of many times in our past when we overreacted or snapped at friends or relatives for offering us unsolicited advice, or we got overly defensive with a stranger or sales clerk for being insensitive to our needs. We might not have run out of the room, but maybe we became confrontational or disagreeable.

Next we'll break down how enacting the relaxation response on a regular basis turns meditation into a washing machine for old, accumulated stress triggers, and how your truest measure of progress is noticing how much less you get triggered into fighting or fleeing as meditation creates a protective shield against tomorrow's high-pressure demands potentially leading to un-merited (and unhealthy) stressful reactions.

EVERY DAY IS LAUNDRY DAY:
WASHING AWAY THE STRESS

De-stressing in meditation is a robust process that helps us purge the backlog of triggers, trauma, and junk that has been hiding in the cellular memory of our bodies for decades. The challenge, though, is that it may cause you to have more thought-filled (rough and rocky) meditation experiences. And many of those thoughts could be related to the very stresses that are being dissolved, or washed out. Likewise, it's not possible for meditation to "launder" your body without at least some strange, possibly unpleasant emotions tainting your mental experiences. Sometimes you'll just have what feels like a busy mind. But as you'll learn, even having a busy mind in meditation can be a healthy symptom of progress! Crazy, I know. But it bears repeating: *Having a busy mind in meditation is a sign of progress.*

Let's suppose you're following the same E.A.S.Y. process, which normally yields a settled-mind experience—except in this meditation, instead of your mind feeling settled like it has in past meditations, it feels more like the grand finale of a Fourth of July fireworks display, as your thoughts are exploding into a dazzling array of associations, sensations, worries, and concerns. Your mind is more active because your body is using the experience of rest to release stress. Your job is to remain passive, remembering that the purpose of de-stressing is so you can feel like the best version of you *outside* of meditation: in the job interview, on the first date, when you're giving the presentation, while driving, when having difficult conversations with your spouse . . . you know, when it really counts.

Reframing the "Monkey Mind" Experience

Whenever you have a meditation where your mind feels exceptionally busy (monkey mind) and you become aware of it, instead of judging the quality of the meditation as bad, try to reframe your experience. Replace "My mind was *too* busy in that meditation" with "Wow, my body just released *a lot of stress!*" Over time, you will begin to naturally celebrate the positive cause (stress release) and not just rebuke the symptom (a busy mind). You will also continue to move away from the misconception that thinking is somehow bad and poses an insurmountable obstacle to a successful meditation.

When it comes to the stress-release phenomenon, there's a good chance that, mixed in with thoughts about your day, you may also experience sensations or unresolved emotions from your distant past. For instance, when it's tax time, you'll likely be thinking about calling your accountant or organizing your finances, and those thoughts will be mixed with a little anxiety from an experience you had a decade ago, plus the thoughts of your Settling Sound and the meditation process. If you had an argument with your spouse earlier that day, you may find yourself thinking about a better way you could've handled that situation, combined with anger from childhood, mixed with a feeling of sleepiness. If you haven't had sex in a while, you may find yourself fantasizing in meditation about a desire for romantic intimacy, while also noticing you feel frustrated about something that happened last week financially, combined with an itchy feeling or slight nausea.

In other words, expect your mind to rehearse and reflect whatever is happening right now, *and* be roaming through the random-thoughts zone, *and* be the exhaust pipe for stress release—particularly in the opening half of your meditation, as your mind is settling. A part of you will want to cling to the old, mistaken, amateur belief that meditation is working only if you're not experiencing unwanted thoughts and sensations. But always remember, it's not an either-or experience. It's *both-and.* Meditation is working *and* you may be experiencing some weird stuff. The weird stuff is not an obstacle but the side effect. In other words, it's both working and sometimes weird.

It's a big ask for beginning meditators who still view their mind as the obstacle to view the thought-, emotion-, and sensation-filled meditation experiences as correct. But by doing so, you'll quickly become a pro meditator because you'll ultimately train your mind to automatically begin settling beyond the unavoidably bizarre thoughts and experiences in spite of the de-stressing process.

De-stressing is an essential and beneficial function of meditation. The feelings that de-stressing evokes may take you by surprise at first, but once you become more familiar with the process, you can more easily embrace, accept, surrender to, and yield to all experiences—and view them as proof that your daily practice is working!

WHEN THE SMOKE CLEARS

I want to share a real-life story of a former meditation student who experienced a particularly bizarre sensation during her initial days of meditation.

Mona was a friend of my mother's from their yoga class, and

she described herself as a "health nut"—a vegetarian bohemian who lived alone and took remarkable care of her health, and had done so for as long as she could remember. She attended one of my first meditation trainings, and afterward she reported having positive experiences and much success settling her mind and body with little effort.

A couple of months after starting, she reached out for an explanation related to a strange experience she had two weeks into her practice. In short, Mona began to taste and smell cigarette smoke during her meditations. The taste and smell were so strong that she was concerned someone was smoking nearby. She kept interrupting her meditations to check if a window was open or if there was smoke somehow entering through a vent. But she saw no evidence of cigarette smoke anywhere around her home, and she even experimented with meditating in her car, to see if the taste and smell would follow her there. Sure enough, when they made an appearance, Mona knew that this was an internal phenomenon. And a few meditations later it ended, just as spontaneously as it had begun.

Initially I suspected that it was related to stress release, but I wanted *her* to make the connection. She assured me that as long as she could remember, she had carefully avoided spending time in any place with exposure to secondhand smoke. I agreed that she was currently living a healthy lifestyle, and began probing throughout her past to see where she had been exposed to cigarettes. I knew it had to be there. We just had to find it.

"Did your parents smoke when you were growing up?"

"No," she answered.

"Have you ever smoked yourself? Think back to when you were a teenager."

A lightbulb went off as she began to remember. "You know, there was a period of time, for maybe six months, when I lived in New York. I was in my early twenties, and I smoked cigarettes on occasion. But that was over forty years ago! Surely it can't be that."

"That's most likely what it is," I assured her. "The meditating physiology is uncanny for its ability to go into the back of the 'closet' and discard old stress that's been long since forgotten about. That's how de-stressing works. You were twenty-one, twenty-two years old at the time, in the big city, meeting so many new people, having so many new experiences, and feeling the insecurities that come with being a young adult. Surely there were some strong emotions swirling in and around your day-to-day interactions. And in the process, your body memorized all the sensations that were present—mainly the taste and smell of cigarette smoke. And now that you're meditating, your body is discarding forty-year-old trash that was hidden away but keeping you bound to your past."

Meditation is as effective a laundering process for old stress triggers as it gets. As Mona experienced, however, the only problem is that when the old stress leaves, it often makes you feel as though you're reexperiencing those same old sensations and emotions again. And because this can muddy your meditations, the only way to know for sure that you're experiencing stress release is to examine how you feel *outside* of meditation.

THE GLENN BECK MEDITATIONS

Sometimes you may be inundated with thoughts about particularly dark subjects, either in one entire meditation or over a string of meditations. I've heard stories of psycho ex-boyfriends, panic attacks, dizzy spells, clowns, vertigo, falling, and even celebrities coming up in people's meditations.

When I first began to check up on Franklin's progress in the first few months after he began learning to meditate, almost every conversation about his experiences would end in a long-winded politically charged rant recounting something that conservative political pundit Glenn Beck said on television that upset him.

A month later I followed up, and once again I noted that Franklin seethed with anger over Beck's political commentary. As it turned out, Franklin couldn't tear himself away from watching Glenn Beck, so I recommended a news fast (which I've had to go on as well from time to time when the tone of the news becomes too sensational). But while it was obvious even to him that watching Fox News made him very angry, he couldn't quit tuning in. Franklin was a die-hard political news junkie, and his viewing habits were firmly ingrained.

He told me how sometimes he would encounter Glenn Beck in his meditations, and it took everything he had not to turn anger toward his mind during his practice. I reminded Franklin that Beck's special appearances in his meditation were symptomatic of his body purging the stress that he had obviously accumulated while spending years obsessively watching Fox News and getting upset—and that's most likely why thoughts and angry emotions related to Glenn Beck appeared to be hijacking his meditations. I encouraged him to not mind those thoughts, to keep being as passive as possible, and to be on the lookout for an upgrade in the quality of his thoughts and experiences *outside* of meditation.

Sure enough, about five months later I checked in with him again, and this time he mentioned nothing about Fox News. I asked him jokingly how his "Glenn Beck meditations" were going. He said he didn't have them anymore. Not only that, but he could now watch Fox News without being emotionally triggered by the content. He realized how the negative emotions he used to feel toward the Fox News commentators were more destructive to him than productive, and how he now felt infinitely more liberated. Incidentally, a few months after that, I checked on him again, and that time he told me he'd stopped watching Fox News.

Like Franklin, you may experience recurring themes in your meditations, perhaps in the form of song lyrics you can't get out of your head, conversations, judgments, sleepiness, or thinking obsessively about a particularly dark memory or "bad" person. Again, these are all common symptoms of your body purging old stress. Your mind is not a mischievous perpetrator out to ruin your meditations. Rather, it's the ultimate release valve during meditation as old stresses are being purged from your body. These often uncomfortable thoughts and odd sensations represent stress you will never have to be affected by again. Stress's ability to hijack your good mood or yank you out of the present moment is being weakened from one meditation to the next.

THE DRANO EFFECT

I used to live alone in a beach cottage near Venice Beach, and one day, out of the blue, my bathroom sink got clogged up. This confused me because I have a shaved head, so I knew it wasn't hair that was causing the stoppage, plus I had a cover over the drain, which meant nothing could've fallen into it. My first attempt to fix it involved going down to the drugstore and getting some Drano. When I poured it into the sink, the situation improved only about 5 percent.

I went to the hardware store and bought the industrial-strength drain opener, with a big skull-and-crossbones warning label on the bottle. The instructions were to wear goggles and gloves, then open the bottle, pour the clear liquid down into the drain, cover the drain with a bowl, and after about thirty minutes run cold water into the sink. I carefully followed the directions, and while pouring the liquid down the drain I heard some sizzling and snapping deep down in the P-trap. Whatever was in there clogging up the sink was definitely getting dissolved.

Then I understood why the instructions said to cover the drain—because a funky odor from the bowels of the drain began wafting throughout my house. I covered the drain with a bowl and took a walk to the coffee shop down the street. When I returned half an hour later and ran cold water into the sink, the blockage had cleared. The industrial-strength drain opening agent worked.

Like the Drano I used first, temporary fixes don't do much to help us permanently release stress. We need something more—something "industrial-strength." Think of rest as a good cleansing agent—it is the basis for helping the body repair itself and restore balance. It is like Kryptonite to the type of stress that causes us to overreact to innocent situations. If we accumulate more stress than rest on a daily basis, then one day, out of the blue, we may notice that our digestive system just stops working, or our joints hurt, or we cannot fall asleep at night. When our body loses its ability to function in a balanced way, stress accumulation is a major indicator, and it can lead to a host of health problems such as heart disease, depression, anxiety, and weight gain.

We may first attempt to sleep more hours, but once you're sleep-deprived, sleeping longer doesn't necessarily equate to getting a better quality of rest. It's been shown that if the restful quality is missing, then the sleep deprivation can worsen over time. In other words, the clog persists. Something stronger and geared to the intelligence of the body is usually required. Meditation has been shown to be the equivalent of the industrial-strength rest agent. How do you know if the meditation is working? The same way I knew my sink had been fixed—afterward I was able to run water down my sink with no blockages. With meditation, the way you know it's working is by whether the mental and physical blockages have cleared. In other words, you can finally sleep at night, your digestive issues diminish, you can get "it" up at night without enhancers, an irritating ache or pain goes away, your body can quickly heal itself if you get sick, you no longer have to run out of the room due to a song playing, and so on.

How you feel outside of meditation is the best way to track your progress with meditation. The worst way to determine progress is to base it on what you thought about *during* meditation. In many instances, the content of your busy-mind thoughts in meditation is symptomatic of what's being dissolved deep down in your proverbial P-trap, where you can't see it, but you can sometimes feel and smell it.

10

MEDICATION VS. MEDITATION

Terry sought out meditation because her twelve-year-old son, Johnny, had an extreme case of attention deficit hyperactivity disorder (ADHD), and his therapist recommended meditation as a way of alleviating it. If meditation could help Johnny even a little, Terry said in an email to me before we met, she would be relieved. Even with medication, she warned me, his outward symptoms could be severe. I invited them out to my orientation so that I could meet Johnny in person (a requirement before agreeing to teach someone who may potentially have special needs), and they attended a training I gave in Miami.

Johnny appeared to be an average preteen, dressed in a loose-fitting Miami Dolphins T-shirt, a baseball cap pulled down over his eyes. Despite some mild fidgeting, he managed to sit through the entire ninety-minute orientation. Judging from my initial casual observations, I was confident that Johnny would be able to succeed in meditation like everyone else, in spite of the concerns his mother expressed about his lack of ability to sit still.

On the first day of the training, Johnny and his mother sat in a room with about nine others. One by one, I took each student aside and gave them their individual mantras (when I teach Vedic meditation in person, I give everyone a personalized mantra suited to their psychophysiology). I purposely waited to give Johnny his mantra last. And then I proceeded to lead them all through the initial steps of using their sounds properly in order to achieve a greater sense of relaxation in their minds and bodies. Then, as he sat with his eyes closed and attempted to use his sound, Johnny began to fidget. His mother, wary of her son's condition, peeked from one eye to make sure he was safe. I could see her growing embarrassment, but no one else knew what was happening because everyone's eyes were closed.

Then Johnny's fidgeting became jolting. He began jumping and jerking as if he was trying to meditate with a mouse crawling around in his pants. I had never seen anything like it.

At certain points I asked the group to stop meditating so I could check in on their experience. Each time we stopped, Johnny would settle down. And when we started up again, he would begin jumping around in his chair like a kernel of corn in a popper. I could tell that he was growing increasingly embarrassed, too. At the end of the session, I didn't mention anything about his jerking and popping. I reassured him and his mother that he was doing just fine, and gave them a couple of homework meditations to practice on their own before returning the next day.

On day two of my training, Johnny told me that his at-home meditation experience was better—he was less jumpy—than what he had felt in the first session. I wasn't all that surprised. Being able to meditate in a room by himself instead of around a bunch of strangers had probably made him less self-conscious; he had not been concerned with anyone thinking he was weird.

At the end of the second session of instruction, we did another group meditation, but this time Johnny's jolts were even more violent. I could tell that he was growing extremely frustrated with his inability to sit still. And his mother was on edge on his behalf, too. At the end of the session, I acknowledged his jumpiness and told him not to worry but rather to try to apply the E.A.S.Y. approach to it all—embrace, accept, surrender, and yield to his antsiness. One of the problems, I explained, was that he was resisting it. And, like trying to hold in a cough, it was coming out more violently for having been repressed. "If you can," I said, "treat the jolting as perfect practice, meaning that if you're not jumping around, then you're not doing it right."

Johnny looked a little stunned, and unsure if I was serious. I assured him that I was. "That is how you are going to move beyond it," I told him. I then asked if he got jumpy when he watched his favorite television show. No, he answered.

"That's because you're engaged in the story," I told him. "With meditation, I want you to fully engage in the process, and if the process includes jolting and jumping, then jump away! Enjoy it. Smile about it."

Johnny returned the next day and reported that his ADHD was increasingly less prevalent in his home practice. His mother confirmed his report. She was slowly becoming a believer in the power of meditation. This was the day that I planned to talk about stress release, and here's what I told the group, with Johnny's situation in mind. "When your body is de-stressing as a result of meditation, you may sometimes feel as though you're reexperiencing stress from your past in the meditation. It's as if the meditation is causing you to feel antsy, frustrated, panicky, or anxious, but actually it's the other way around. Your previous antsiness, anxiety, and frustration are being purged from your body, and that is what is making you feel antsy during your meditation. How do you know this is the case—that feeling something seemingly negative in meditation indicates that it's leaving the body, and not entering it? You'll know it based on how you feel *outside* of the meditation, once it's over. And gradually you'll notice that while you may be feeling jumpy as you meditate, you're becoming less anxious in your life outside of the meditation."

Johnny was hanging on to every word. Then it was time for us to meditate. I went to Johnny and reminded him that the jolts he'd been experiencing in meditation were probably a mixture of his body de-stressing anxiety and his resistance to having the anxiety in the first place. I reminded him to flip his self-assessment to pleasure and acceptance, and this time see how high he could jump out of his seat. I suggested that he celebrate the ADHD like he was at a party. "Lean into it," I told him. "And if you still experience it, you know it's indeed stress being released, which means less ADHD that you'll have to deal with tomorrow."

Then we all sat to meditate, and Johnny didn't move an inch the entire twenty minutes! He was perfectly still and relaxed. Later he pulled me aside and asked, "Why didn't you just give me those instructions in the beginning?"

"Because," I explained, "you wouldn't have believed me unless you had the jumpy experiences first. Now you have the contrast in your experiences, and you see what it feels like to reject your condition versus embrace it."

Johnny finished the training, and his mother updates me from time to time, letting me know that he's still meditating and experiencing less ADHD outside of meditation, which was the overall goal. I'm not suggesting that someone like Johnny throw out his medication and replace it with meditation, but clearly, its stress-release benefits improved his quality of life.

As I cautioned in the very beginning of this book, if you've been taking any medications, it's best not to discontinue them simply because you started meditating. As we delve into the more dramatic reports of meditators who have experienced physical benefits from meditating, it's tempting to give meditation *all* the credit. But like the aforementioned 2013 Super Bowl champs, there were certainly other important factors that played a role in the Seahawks' success: practice, coaching, recruiting, and so on. In the case of George, whose story we'll get to later in this chapter, the benefits were more likely a result of the medications he was taking combined with the rest he acquired from his consistent meditation practice (emphasis on "consistent"). The next report is from Cole, who actively sought out meditation as a possible solution to a very real and potentially deadly health crisis.

NATURE'S REJECTION IS NATURE'S PROTECTION

For as long as Cole can remember, his passion has been coaching college basketball. Over the last eight years, he has worked his way up the assistant basketball coach ladder, first at a West Coast school, then at a Midwest college, and currently at a large university in the South.

I met Cole just after he saw a doctor for dyshidrosis—itchy feet. His doctor gave him a routine blood pressure check, and noticed the reading was unusually high for someone who was only twenty-seven—150 over 80 (a systolic reading between 140 and 159 is considered stage 1 hypertension).

When Cole filled his doctor in on the daily pressures of coaching Division I basketball—the frequent outbursts, the deep disappointments linked to the high stakes, the emotionally charged environment of games, the practices and recruiting efforts—the picture became clearer. Cole was well on his way toward dangerous chronic hypertension, his doctor warned him, and a few more weeks of careful monitoring confirmed the diagnosis.

The doctor offered Cole three options: (1) begin aggressive drug treatment therapy and, because he was having to do so at such a young age, be prepared for adverse side effects later in life; (2) retire from coaching and find less stressful (less life-threatening) work; or (3) seek out a form of meditation that would increase his ability to manage the inevitable stress and challenges that came with his job—and control his blood pressure.

Even though he had never even considered meditating a day in his life, retirement and a lifetime of pharmaceutical drugs were so unacceptable that Cole felt meditation was his only real choice. He did some online research and eventually tracked me down. In his first email to me, he admitted he had no clue about meditation, but wanted to know if it could help him better manage his accumulated stress.

I'm always wary of making guarantees, especially without meeting someone in person first, because aside from improved sleep, I never like to speculate about how a new meditator will benefit from meditation, especially with regard to physical benefits. Over the years, I've seen how factors such as consistency of practice, genetics, diet, lifestyle, and positive mindset all play a key role in physical, mental, and spiritual transformation. While I couldn't guarantee to Cole what his results would be, I told him that I could help take all of the guesswork out of meditation. That would put him in the best possible position to release stress—and as we know by now, whenever our bodies have an opportunity to release more stress than they take on each day, our health tends to improve.

I told Cole I'd had experience teaching people with high blood pressure, and discussed the link to sleep deprivation, along with other inexplicable health issues, such as his itchy feet. Then I explained the meaningful exchange, and Cole initially balked—

but concluded that comprehensive instruction and a lifetime of support from me (I regularly check in with every student I train—for as long as they'll have me) was still cheaper than going on medication, and if meditation could really help lower his blood pressure, it would be money well spent. He was willing to commit.

Within days of beginning his meditation training, Cole reported to me that he had noticed his sleep improve remarkably (an unexpected benefit). At the suggestion of his doctor, he bought a blood pressure cuff and tracked his progress by regularly measuring his blood pressure after meditation. He did this each morning like clockwork, usually on the couch in his bedroom.

Cole would sit for his twenty-minute meditation by 7:40 every morning, and again before afternoon team practice. On rare days when he had a meeting with a player before practice, he would meditate later in the evening before dinner. He also began incorporating a gratitude exercise into his practice, where he would list ten different things in his life that he was grateful for after each meditation. I was inspired to hear that he was taking more of an integrative approach to his healing and not putting all the pressure on his meditation practice. But I consider meditation to be one of the key habits that makes it easier to do the other things that add to a more balanced life (expressing gratitude, exercising, eating well, and more).

Throughout his first year, Cole got into meditation so thoroughly and was able to settle so deeply that once someone came right up and poked his shoulder to make sure he was alive! He also reported that he was able to meditate through his nieces and nephews jumping on him during a family visit. And, embarrassingly, he overmeditated a few times and was late to practice. But it was all worth it, because in his first year of meditation Cole saw his blood pressure drop out of the red zone—down to 135 over 70—without taking one pill. Even his doctor was amazed that it happened so quickly.

But what Cole was most inspired by was how much his outlook on life evolved with meditation. He began seeing the world from a broader perspective and described himself as kinder, gentler, and more understanding in all areas of life. He took to heart one of the mottos he heard me repeat in the training: "Nature's rejection is nature's protection," which means that if something isn't going your way (relationships, the outcome of games, traffic, etc.), it wasn't meant to be, or better yet, you're being spared from experiencing something worse. Cole began to see that when his players or other coaches irritated him, they were simply doing their best or behaving the way they themselves had been conditioned; Cole realized that no amount of his own reaction would necessarily change their behavior.

Although Cole still has stressful days—as he has become more successful, his job has become more demanding—overall he describes himself as being more self-aware and mindful of his daily interactions. The anger he occasionally experiences doesn't linger as long. If he fails to sign a new recruit or sees one of his players making a mistake, it no longer ruins his entire day or week. And physically he is healthier and stronger—very different from how he felt when he first sought me out.

Cole's meditation practice remains a constant in his busy life, and he can count on both hands the number of days he's missed in five years. He's also meditated enough to realize that there are no good or bad meditations, that it's just something you do, like brushing your teeth. Cole still doesn't mention to his players that he meditates (which was why I didn't list the schools where he coaches). But he enjoys the credit he gets for the creative offenses that usually occur to him while deep in meditation. (In meditation jargon, we refer to those types of insights as "cognitions"—we'll examine them in Chapter 11.)

THE GEORGE REPORTS

Whether I'm teaching in a corporate office or at someone's home, it's easy for passersby to recognize that a meditation session is in progress by the sea of shoes strewn about near the entrance. It's such an obvious sign of what to do when you arrive (take your shoes off) that I'm always surprised when some people enter the teaching space with their shoes still on.

Removing shoes is mainly a carryover from the ancient Indian custom of only entering a temple or ashram with bare feet—a tradition I've been observing ever since I first began studying with my teacher. Everyone *must* remove his or her shoes before entering the room. That's just how it is.

I've met thousands of people teaching meditation, and a handful of them stand out—perhaps because they shared a mind-blowing personal story, showed up insanely late, heckled me during my presentation, were very funny or quirky, or offered me a truly generous contribution as their exchange for teaching them (or they drastically low-balled me—like the guy who once paid me with $20 and a how-to book on origami).

George stood out for his own unique reason: he refused to remove his shoes. George was a tall, gangly African American man of Trinidadian descent who looked to be in his midsixties. The evening he first arrived at my orientation, he entered the room wearing dark-colored slacks and a red-checkered button-down shirt, a blazer, and thick-soled black shoes. Removing his shoes wasn't an option, he told my assistant, who quietly gestured to me. I made my way through the crowd to greet the man who started the training with defiance—not the mark of a good student. After a warm handshake, George apologized profusely but explained that for nearly a decade, due to a metatarsal problem, he'd worn orthopedic shoes to walk pain-free. If he took off his shoes at the door, he wouldn't even be able to walk the fifteen steps to his seat. This was a reasonable explanation, so I made an exception and he was very grateful. When he reached his chair, he removed his shoes and settled in for my talk.

George was intrigued by the way I presented meditation during my orientation, and when we had a chance to meet again privately after the session, he revealed more details about his journey leading up to that night. He had considerable health problems, including gastrointestinal issues made worse after his former dentist put him on a round of aggressive antibiotics. George's daughter had encouraged him to seek help from a naturopathic doctor in order to receive herbal treatment for his stomach ailments. But the naturopath, understanding the interconnectedness of the body, recommended that George first learn how to meditate before receiving the treatment. The doctor suspected that some of George's digestive imbalances were stress-related, and knew that his herbal remedies would be a lot more effective if George was managing his stress better. George heard about my training and registered for the orientation.

Undoubtedly, part of George's stress could be attributed to his lifestyle: he was a struggling playwright in Chicago who had ridden the arts roller coaster, complete with financial and creative ups and downs, for decades. George looked forward to learning a practice that would help him combat the accumulated stress of his feast-or-famine career choice, and after meeting me he quickly determined that meditation was the answer. He showed up early to each session, and every time I allowed him to walk to his chair first and then remove his shoes.

As always, I encouraged the meditators-in-training to engage completely in allowing their minds to roam during meditation. You know by now (from experience) that learning to let your mind wander and eventually get lost is easier said than done, and ends up being one of the most challenging aspects of learning this approach to meditation. But George was a natural at roaming. He credited his extensive acting training with teaching him to embrace stream-of-consciousness thinking. In fact, he could relate to my position as his teacher, because for years he'd taught acting classes where he spent a good part of the semester encouraging his students to surrender fully to their stream of consciousness.

George completed the course extremely enthusiastic about

his new daily meditation practice. As with many of my early students, I would make a point to check in with them on a weekly basis to answer questions, make sure they were receiving all of the benefits from the practice that they could, and offer reminders and inspiration. George would regularly respond with his own reports from the field.

Report from the Field: The Unexpected Benefit

For years I've had a serious problem with my left foot, and have had tremendous difficulty walking, especially in bare feet. I've spent a fortune buying orthopedic shoes. But they never helped much. Then I began meditating. I had expected to feel less stressed and to sleep better, but I never expected that my chronic pain would be impacted as well. About three weeks after I began meditating, I was vacuuming and not really paying much attention to how I felt physically—and then I looked down and realized I was walking on my bare feet pain-free. I always suspected my pain was psychosomatic, but I was unsure because it was so physical for so many years.

—George

But that was just the beginning. Here are more "George reports," taken from his emails, regarding additional physical benefits he experienced. All of these improvements came about after around three years of daily meditation.

Anyone who suffers from hypertension understands how amazing this breakthrough is. I've been battling my blood pressure for ten years, and taking medication for it as well. At one point the readings had gone up significantly, as high as 170/90, which is close to borderline for "hit the panic button." Two doctors wanted me to either increase the meds I was taking or change to a different drug. One day I was trying to figure out why I froze up every time I had to have my pressure taken, and remembered the "white coat phenomenon." I suddenly realized an amazingly simple truth: I was afraid of failing the test! Once I understood that, it resonated. Now the numbers are down to 130/60, 140/75, 138/70!

Disclosure: I'm seeing an acupuncturist and it's helping, but when I went to him my level was still hitting 166/80. No natural herb is going to reduce blood pressure that dramatically in someone who's been taking a drug for it as long as I have. It's definitely the meditation. I'm now working up to being able to get off the drugs completely.

Next, he reported a surprise change in his back pain:

My back pain has become a thing of the past and I think meditation gets the credit. I know that my energy is improving in many ways from what it was fifteen years ago. I've been 99 percent consistent for the entire three years. It's been such a boon in so many ways.

And finally, George saw improvement in what he originally sought out meditation to help heal:

> I came to meditation originally because a dentist had ruined my stomach by prescribing too many antibiotics. Now, it's taken me three years, but I think meditation finally solved my gut problem. If that is indeed the case, then I can die happy.

After reading the reports from Cole and George, you may be tempted to hope that you might have similar benefits, particularly if you've suffered from an illness or injury and conventional approaches don't seem to be working. However, as far as I've seen, meditation benefits can be very individual. Also, these reports are from meditators who were trained in my live Vedic meditation class—utilizing similar principles outlined in this book but with the added benefit of having personal contact with me, as well as regular follow-up support. In addition to that, each made a meaningful exchange, which I also believe played an important role in their level of commitment. Overall, it's best to keep your expectations low and commitment high when starting out in meditation. If and when the bigger benefits occur, you'll be pleasantly surprised.

HOW TO KNOW IF MEDITATION IS WORKING FOR YOU

Here I want to offer you more common indicators of progress that aren't as remarkable as what Cole and George reported.

Still, when added together, these smaller benefits lead to a significantly higher quality of life, and are also linked to a consistent meditation practice:

- You don't get sick as often.
- You recover from illness faster.
- You digest your food better.
- You have an increased amount of patience.
- You feel physically stronger (your athletic performance may improve).
- Women may have more regular menstrual cycles.
- You sleep better at night.
- Illnesses may go into remission.
- You become less confrontational, argumentative, and disagreeable.
- You find it easier to empathize with others.
- You develop a healthier appetite, with less binge eating.
- You feel more rested upon awakening.
- Your dreams are more vivid.
- Sensations seem richer.
- Time seems to slow down enough for you to enjoy small moments.
- You stop and smell the flowers more often.
- You become a better listener.
- You communicate more effectively.
- You think more clearly.
- You have more present-moment awareness.
- You can "see around the corner" easier.

- You don't take things as personally.
- You are able to laugh at yourself more.

If any of these real-world benefits are occurring, then your meditation is working beautifully, in spite of what it feels like *inside* the meditations. It's also not unusual to have a thought-filled meditation on the heels of a good night's rest. Or to fall asleep in meditation, yet feel extremely alert during the 2:00-to-4:00 p.m. slump when everyone at the office is going for their second or third coffee of the day.

Long-term meditators know from experience that meditation is often a game of seemingly unrelated contradictions, where you feel as though you're backsliding in one moment, but you're actually progressing. It's fun (and eye-opening) to note how different the inner experience can be from the outer experience.

11

STUMBLING UPON A COGNITION

Harriet was working as a hospital administrator in New York City when we met. A former nurse, she attended my training after reading about the health benefits of meditation and the ways in which it can help to improve mental clarity. In the session when I usually cover the benefits of de-stressing, the new meditators went around and shared their experiences. Here is what Harriet reported from earlier that day.

An energetic intern in her busy office wanted to start an initiative to help upgrade the overall patient experience at the hospital. He met with various administrators throughout the day to seek counsel, and one by one, they explained to the intern that although what he was trying to accomplish was noble, it simply wasn't possible; they had all tried it before, and due to office politics, lack of funding, and no support from senior-level administrators, the proposal would never get off the ground. The young intern was hitting a brick wall with every administrator he sought out, each of whom voiced essentially the same reasons for why his plan wouldn't work. But the intern refused to give up.

Harriet, normally optimistic, quietly agreed that the intern's proposal was indeed impossible, and she began mentally rehearsing how she could artfully let him down without dampening his spirit. When the persistent intern made his way over to Harriet's cubicle and solicited her advice for moving his idea forward, to Harriet's astonishment, she witnessed herself begin to explain to the intern, in detail, exactly how to execute his "impossible" proposal.

"Call this person," she told him, "and have them sign off on a budget of X amount, then get their colleague involved. To attract them to the project, make sure to mention this aspect of it, and then go and talk to this other person, and tell them who's involved," et cetera. She laid out the entire plan, and it actually sounded plausible—even to her.

At the same time, she wondered to herself, "Where in the hell did that come from?" Her plan worked, but she needed to know what kind of special powers the meditation had instilled within her after only three days.

She had had a "cognition," I explained to Harriet and the rest of the class. A cognition is a fairly common symptom of regularly settling your mind in meditation. The first time you have one, it may feel like luck. The second time, it feels like a weird coincidence. But by the tenth time you have a cognition, you know that something extraordinary is going on, as you keep getting these intuitive hits and creative downloads seemingly out of the blue. That Harriet's advice was spontaneous—meaning it wasn't predetermined, yet it was the *right* solution to an old problem—is a classic indicator of a meditation-generated cognition. Cognitions may originate within the meditation, but very often you won't articulate the creative idea or epiphany until you're back in action, and often right when you need it. Yet during the meditation you could've been thinking about something as random as making popcorn or contemplating how the pyramids were constructed, along with other unrelated thoughts, which makes cognitions seem few and far between in the beginning days of meditating. Now is a good time to examine what those other thoughts are, and why you have them.

THE FOUR MOST COMMON TYPES OF THOUGHTS IN MEDITATION

Here I've distilled the most common thoughts you'll have during meditation into four main categories:

- Roaming thoughts (unrelated to the awareness that you're meditating)
- Stress-release thoughts (distressful thoughts of any kind)
- Analytical thoughts (obsessive thinking)
- Solution-oriented thoughts (cognitions, positive thoughts, or insights)

This does not mean you will experience only one of the types of thoughts exclusively during meditation. Most likely you will be experiencing one, two, three, or all four simultaneously. One type may be dominant, while the rest could be background experiences. And *any* of these four types of thoughts could be experienced while mentally roaming, de-stressing, starting, or finishing your meditations.

Roaming Thoughts

As you may remember, your mind should begin to roam soon after you begin passively thinking the Settling Sound. Roaming thoughts are *any* thoughts that are unrelated to the awareness that you're meditating. Roaming indicates that your mind is meandering toward the settling zone. These thoughts could include content about literally anything as your mind wanders and drifts toward the settled state. But usually they are about what is happening around you as you're meditating, followed by thoughts regarding short-term or long-term past and future experiences, followed by dream-like fantasies and imaginings.

While roaming, your mind may drift from thought to thought in a seemingly unrelated, unfocused fashion—similar to "gathering your thoughts" while lying in bed. Any surface-mind thinking (including thoughts about surrounding noises and to-do lists) or subtle-mind thinking (including dreamy thoughts like shapes, colors, sounds, transcendent feelings, floating, lights, and numbness) can be considered a roaming experience. The way you know that roaming has begun is that you'll be thinking about something random and simultaneously forget that you're meditating. In other words, if you are aware that you're roaming *while* you're roaming, you're not actually roaming.

The roaming mind will feel like this:

"Ahhh-huummm . . . ahhh-huummmm . . ."

"What's for dinner . . . ?"

"Macaroni and cheese . . . ?"

"I love Robert De Niro movies . . ."

"I need to make a dental appointment . . ."

"My teeth are like the Earth . . ."

"My toes are like the stars . . ."

"It feels so nice to float . . ."

Stress-Release Thoughts

Stress-release thoughts, also referred to as de-stressing thoughts, are any thoughts, emotions, or sensations that feel inherently negative. They can occur inside or outside of meditation. As discussed in Chapter 9, de-stressing is often related to past or future experiences, or to negative feelings associated with the meditation process.

You know you are having de-stressing thoughts when you find yourself getting frustrated by your inability to meditate with ease and effortlessness. You feel physically uncomfortable, no matter how many times you adjust your position. You fall asleep, or start to cry, laugh uncontrollably, grow angry, or become fearful. You may get extremely bored. You may also feel sensations of heaviness, heat, cold, itchy skin, racing heart, headaches, nausea, dizziness, or pressure in your head or body. De-stressing makes your mind unusually active in meditation, despite your being E.A.S.Y. in your technique. When you realize you're meditating, there is a strong temptation to take your negative thoughts or experiences personally, as if there is something wrong with you, or you are incapable of meditating.

All de-stressing (negative feelings, thoughts, emotions, etc.) represents a release of stress from the body, which is one of the most positive outcomes of meditation. The best way to deal with or diminish de-stressing thoughts or sensations as they occur in meditation is to stay E.A.S.Y.

The de-stressing mind "sounds" like this:

"Ahhh-huummm . . . ahhh-huummmm . . ."

"I'm tired of cooking . . ."

"No one appreciates it anyway . . ."

"I hate Robert De Niro movies . . ."

"I hate the dentist, too . . ."

"Plus they're way too expensive . . ."

"I just got really hot all of a sudden . . . !"

"Meditation isn't working today. Either that, or I'm just not good at it . . ."

Analytical Thoughts

Analytical thoughts, also known as "mind-racing" thoughts, usually occur when your mind is attempting to problem-solve for you in meditation. Generally speaking, analytical thoughts are centered around a recent problem, challenge, or demand. Analytical thoughts often result in a cognition (a solution, a good idea, or a welcome insight) either in that same meditation or maybe hours or days later.

The most common feeling associated with analytical thoughts

is the experience of your mind speeding up, or noticing a rapid-fire barrage of related thoughts, mainly fixated on one situation or problem. You feel like your mind won't turn off no matter what adjustments you make or how E.A.S.Y. you remain. These thoughts often occur if you meditate after an argument, or after experiencing a change of expectation that may alter your life dramatically (it's not necessary to avoid meditation after trauma, because remember, your mind is working on your behalf to help you cope). It's common to obsess over the change, why it happened, what it means, and what to do about it. But it is not important to assess whether or not you are experiencing analytical thoughts even if you are experiencing them. Allow yourself to remain process-oriented instead of outcome-oriented; in other words, resist the temptation to actively look for solutions.

Remember, whenever your mind is racing in meditation, it is busy working *for* you, not against you. As with stress-release thoughts, the important way to interact with analytical thoughts is to stay E.A.S.Y.

The analyzing mind moves like this:

"Ahhh-huummm . . . ahhh-huummmm . . ."

"What's for dinner . . . ? Macaroni and cheese . . . ?"

"Wait, I'm gluten-free now. I can't have macaroni . . ."

"But there has to be gluten-free macaroni . . ."

"What if I don't find any . . . ?"

"How will I eat macaroni from now on . . . ?"

"Whole Foods is too expensive. Maybe I can make it from scratch . . . ?"

Solution-Oriented Thoughts

A really elegant way to deal with a problem. The million-dollar idea. The perfect song lyric, the opening for your book, the missing plot point in your screenplay, or the ideal response to a question that confused you in a work email. Solution-oriented thoughts, also known as cognitions, provide you with the answers to problems, or creative insights, mainly in the form of epiphanies, great ideas, or a new perspective. Like with Harriet's experience, a cognition can occur to you spontaneously either inside or outside of meditation, and seemingly out of nowhere, meaning you weren't actively studying the problem when it occurred. And oftentimes the answer feels like it was channeled from a "higher" source.

Solution-oriented thoughts also include the replaying of conversations to determine what you should have said, sexual fantasies, and a way of living that inspires you, in addition to loving thoughts, emotions, or deeds that you want to perform. Plus, they include happy memories, creativity, and the feeling of luck and good fortune.

Generally speaking, when solution-oriented thoughts begin to occur, it is very tempting to want to write them down, actively ponder them, or contemplate how to incorporate them into your life—especially if you have a tendency to forget things easily. But a large part of your practice is to continue being E.A.S.Y., even with cognitions. I train my meditators who may be worried about forgetting cognitions to apply what I call the twenty-minute test, meaning that if they can remember the cognition *after* the meditation, then they should by all means take action. If they can't, it probably wasn't worth their time or attention. In other words, treat your memory as the filter for determining whether a cognition is worthy of remembering and acting on.

The mind arriving at a solution-oriented thought might go something like this:

"Ahhh-huummm . . . ahhh-huummmm . . ."

"What's for dinner . . . ? Macaroni and cheese . . . ?"

"I love Robert De Niro movies . . ."

"I need to make a dental appointment . . ."

"My teeth are like the Earth . . ."

"My toes are like the stars . . ."

"That's how I can save money on my trip! I'll get a ticket connecting through Atlanta, but I won't take my connecting flight. I'll just get off in Atlanta and save $300. Genius!"

Now that you know about the various categories of thoughts in meditation, you'll naturally be tempted to tag your experiences as they are happening. "Oh, I think that was a solution-oriented thought," you may say to yourself while meditating. If this happens, just remind yourself to remain E.A.S.Y., which means to be passive with the tagging as well, and let go of the need to know which thought was which. This will become much easier with practice. Next, Alphonso, an IT professional in his thirties, describes his experiences with the various types of thoughts.

Report from the Field: Going to the Movies

I have two types of meditation experiences I'd like to share. The first I call "short nothingness" meditations—physically relaxing sessions where twenty minutes feel like two minutes. It feels like my brain is off (for lack of a better term). I come out of these meditations feeling a little confused but noticeably lighter in spirit and demeanor. After the short nothingness meditations, my sources of stress seem small and unimportant. I often transition from this experience to having a cup of tea in silence or watching the hustle and bustle of the people outside my apartment window.

My second type of meditation is nearly as calming but in a totally different way. I call this experience "the movie of random memories." While being still, breathing, and saying my [Settling Sound], I slip into vivid memories of seemingly random moments in my life—especially childhood. Recently I've recalled a completely suppressed memory of being verbally harassed by a police officer in my late teens. I spent the rest of those twenty minutes truly analyzing the long-lasting effect of that moment and how it changed how I view the world and how I feel about myself and others. It was a lightbulb moment that ended with me exhaling and telling myself to "let that shit go."

Some of these "movies" have been joyful moments that I thought were totally forgotten and that I was glad to recall, though others might yield regrets or sorrow. Either way, I come out of these sessions feeling more awake and aware than I did when I went in. I feel like I understand myself a little more and am able to apply this self-knowledge to my current and future decisions. These are the sessions I am most thankful for.

Meditation has not only helped me to discover the core elements of who I am, but also to understand my emotional connection to forgotten moments, creative triumphs, and fear-based decisions. It has changed me from someone who asks for answers into someone who knows to listen for them.

—Alphonso

WHEN YOU HIT A MEDITATION PLATEAU

It happens. There's a day coming when you're going to think: "Uh-oh, meditation is no longer working." Congratulations— you hit your first meditation plateau. It's not a question of *if* the plateau feeling is going to happen. Don't worry, it's on the way.

After practicing for a few months, the meditators I've trained often notice that they are not going as deep as often. In fact, some have reported having a string of meditations where they feel like they're literally just sitting there, thinking about the fact that they're staring at the inside of their eyelids. "Nothing's happening," they'll say. Sometimes this may last for a good couple of weeks, in other cases for longer.

The meditation plateau is a very common occurrence with long-term meditators. It doesn't mean you've been doing anything wrong or that your process is stalled. In fact, these plateaus happen from time to time for good reasons:

1. Your mind and body are normalizing the experience of "settling," or . . .

2. You're experiencing heavy pockets of stress release, or . . .

3. You're about to get a big burst of creativity due to your mind racing, or . . .

4. All of the above.

During plateaus, more than at any other time in your meditation practice, it's important to be patient and stay consistent. Once you get to the other side of the plateau, you're going to find that your mind is getting more settled than ever before, and it was all worth it.

Sometimes you'll feel flush with settled-mind experiences, and sometimes it feels like your meditation is a bust and your mind is all over the place. When you're in the throes of de-stressing, you think you'll never be able to right the ship again. But keep going, and you'll get back to a point where meditation never felt better. You are on the brink of uncovering a diamond mine of inner experiences so powerful that, in hindsight, it will be apparent that there were never *any* throwaway meditations. They all add to the new and improved body, mind, and perspective.

It Will Pass

One day a meditator returned to the ashram where she had learned meditation, seeking an audience with her teacher.

When it was finally her turn, she entered a room and saw her teacher sitting with his eyes closed. Not wanting to take up too much of her teacher's time, the student skipped the small talk and said, "Teacher, my meditations have been horrible! I feel so distracted, I'm constantly falling asleep, I'm having so many thoughts. It's just horrible! I really need help, as I'm not sure that meditation is working anymore, or maybe I'm doing something wrong—"

The teacher cut her off by raising his hand, and after a beat, he opened his eyes and said matter-of-factly, "Don't worry about it . . . it will pass." Then he closed his eyes and dropped back into his meditative state, while the student walked away disappointed that she didn't get the guidance she was seeking.

A week later, she returned to see her teacher, but this time her entire tune had changed: "Teacher, ever since I came here to see you, my meditations have been quite wonderful! My mind has become so settled, I feel so aware, so peaceful, and so alive! It's just amazing and—"

Again the teacher held up his hand, cutting off his enthusiastic student, and after a pause, he said in the same matter-of-fact tone, "Don't worry . . . it will pass."

The "It'll pass" attitude is the hallmark of a pro meditator who understands (from experience) that it's not possible to sit every day, twice a day, for ten to twenty minutes, engaging in the E.A.S.Y. meditation technique, and *not* benefit from it on some level. As your meditation practice matures, your experiences will continue to refine and evolve into a feeling that is quite indescribable. You won't even realize how impossible it will be to describe the complexity of your experiences until someone who has never meditated asks you, "What has meditation done for you?" You may not be able to articulate it perfectly, but you'll be thinking, "Gosh, it's done so much, you just have to try it for yourself!"

In fact (and unfortunately), the clearest benefits can only be demonstrated when life isn't going as planned. Instead of reacting to protect your ego, your knee-jerk response may be, "Hmmm, there's a good chance that what just happened to me occurred for some higher or divine purpose. Although I may not be able to see it right now, I'm going to do my best to adapt, and be open to the possibility that something good will come of it" (nature's rejection is nature's protection).

There will likely be many baffling thoughts and emotional experiences both inside and outside of meditation, due to the process of maturation. Understand that the process is dynamic, and that nothing—good or bad—will last forever. As you're going through the heavier experiences, remember the story of the wise meditation teacher and keep reminding yourself, "It will pass."

THE EMAIL TEST

I'd like to end this chapter with a fun and extremely effective real-time experiment that you can conduct anytime you want to demonstrate the mental benefits of your meditation practice. I call it the Meditate First/Send Later Email Test. All you need is access to email (probably easiest) or text, or you can just use a conversation you've been mulling over (you'll see how this works in a moment).

If you're like me, you've received a prickly message or had a testy conversation recently, where the other person misinterpreted something you did or said, and . . . let's just say they didn't meditate before sending you their message telling you all the things that are wrong with you or your approach to the situation. And maybe you found their words defensive, obstructive, passive-aggressive, selfish, or insulting.

If you're like me, maybe you've been tempted to fire back one of those "How dare you speak to me like that" messages that perfectly demonstrates your greater understanding of the situation and even your spiritual superiority. If you haven't yet responded, here's what I suggest you do to test the powers of your meditation in real time:

1. Select the offensive email, text message, or recent verbal exchange to respond to. Make sure you pick one that left you feeling depleted or angry—one you are still ruminating over because you haven't yet come up with the perfect response.

2. Go ahead and write out your response (or a script for what you'd say). Feel free to edit as much as you need to make sure it's exactly what you want to communicate, but *do not* press send and do not pick up the phone and call the person with your script in hand.

3. Sit for your next scheduled meditation right away if possible. Granted, you may spend the entire meditation de-stressing or mind-racing with ideas for responding to the sender's message, so be ready with your E.A.S.Y. attitude.

4. Post-meditation, go back and reread your reply, and edit as needed.

5. Hit send, or call them up and have that conversation from a clearer mental state.

You will notice how you upgrade your message to suit your post-meditation, rested state of mind—which generally means you will be able to empathize more easily, or have more compassion in your response. The best part is you can be sitting in meditation thinking roaming thoughts (for instance, what your favorite toy was as a child, or what you want to have for dinner), and still come out with greater clarity around how to respond to the contentious message from a more expansive place. The saying "Let me go meditate on it" is real . . . just don't go into the meditation thinking of solutions. Let your meditation work for you, instead of you working to actively conjure up solutions in meditation.

JOHN KLOSSNER THE NEW YORKER COLLECTION/THE CARTOON BANK

"Maybe you shouldn't send out e-mails when you're tired."

12

THE ART OF BEING ADAPTABLE

There's a popular Internet meme that says, "Did you really have a bad day? Or was it a bad five minutes that you milked all day?" One thing is certain about life: it is ever-changing, demanding, and unpredictable. With consistency, you'll find that your meditation practice will allow you to more easily drop into a "flow state" where you become supremely adaptable to change. You will gradually become a person:

- Who remains cool as a fan when all hell breaks loose
- Who says the insightful thing that your friends repeat to others (and post on social media) because it resonated with them so much
- Who's not taking everything personally
- Who's empathetic toward other people's situations

- Who's forgiving
- Who can keep their mouth shut when they have nothing positive to say
- Who's sleeping through the night and waking up feeling refreshed and happy to be alive
- Who's able to be prospective in addition to retrospective
- And, most important, who's patient (in traffic, in the checkout line, in general)

In short, you will have developed the ability to *adapt*—and that is a powerful skill that will get you through many a challenging moment.

OVERCOMING STICKS AND STONES

Jennifer, an artist in her sixties, found me after having learned meditation with the Transcendental Meditation organization when she was just a young girl. She practiced diligently throughout her teenage years and into college. Then adult life happened, and she fell off the wagon.

Jennifer's interest in meditation was renewed after reading Deepak Chopra's *Life After Death*, and she sought out a local teacher. She attended my training and began practicing again. We stayed in touch, and exactly three years later she sent me the following report about an offensive incident she experienced while walking to her sculpture class, and how she responded to it:

I want to share an experience that demonstrates how far I've come.

This semester I am taking sculpting classes at a community college. I live nearby so I walk back and forth with my heavy supplies. Last Tuesday, I was walking on the sidewalk to class and a guy riding his bike (on the sidewalk) was racing toward me. I moved out of his way to avoid colliding and as he whizzed past, he said, "Out of my way, you fat bitch!"

I was shocked at first—but I was surprised, too, because it didn't hit that place in my upper chest, by my heart, where you get that sinking feeling of the fight/flight response kicking in. I was simply stunned and was trying to figure out what that was all about. Then I thought, "Well, at least he didn't call me a fat 'cow' or fat 'old' bitch." I thought about it so little that it never hurt my feelings. Instead, I interpreted it as a wake-up call from "Nature" to get fit and stay healthy as I'm aging; and that's a good thing. Now that's a major improvement from how I would've handled it three years ago, before I returned to my meditation.

Jennifer's story is as much about her consistency as a meditator as it is about her experience of a real-world benefit of her practice. In a way, her story is refreshing, because this is the type of stuff that happens to all of us from time to time—hearing insensitive comments and taking them personally. You will never read in a meditation study about how meditation minimizes our reaction to such comments. But this is exactly what I want to encourage you to look for in your daily practice to help you gauge the effectiveness of meditation. Are you adapting to the little stuff of life with more grace and ease? If so, then no matter what else is happening *inside* of your meditations, you're right on track.

Here's the thing, though—let's not overlook Jennifer's *three* years of consistent practice. If you're just beginning, three years sounds like a long time from now. But three years is going to fly by anyway, whether you are consistent in your meditation or not. So you may as well be consistent, and you too will reap these types of real-world benefits during that time.

Being adaptable also means you gain a broader perspective on the offensive behaviors of others. It allows you to feel a tangible thread of connection and have more compassion. Maybe the mean-spirited biker just learned his parent is sick. Or perhaps he didn't grow up in a caring family. Maybe he's ashamed of his *own* body. Regardless, the biker didn't know Jennifer, and therefore taking his comment personally would've been an overreaction on Jennifer's part—one that she, not the biker, would ultimately pay the price for in stored-up stress. These types of overreactions, which may feel frequent and normal to you today, will minimize over time with consistent practice of meditation. And as you have future run-ins with antagonistic people, even if the episodes rattle you in the moment, you'll notice how the severity of the impact diminishes faster and faster, and how easily you can return to your new, adaptable state of being.

SPOTTING THE SILVER LINING

Janice's experience is another example of what it looks like when you become more adaptable as a result of your daily practice.

Janice is a realtor whose stress levels and insomnia drove her to my meditation training. Nothing else was able to cure her years-long insomnia curse. After only a couple of days of consistent meditation, however, she finally began experiencing the deep nighttime rest that had eluded her for a decade.

Two weeks later, Janice bumped into a colleague at a work event—another realtor with whom she had developed a very contentious relationship over the years. She had despised this woman for so long that she couldn't even remember why she started hating her in the first place. To Janice, something about the woman was just offensive—perhaps her know-it-all attitude or her primness. She couldn't quite put her finger on it.

This time, though, when Janice encountered her nemesis, she noticed how the usual contempt that she was so accustomed to feeling had mysteriously vanished. But Janice also noticed that a part of her (the old pattern) still wanted to hate the woman! So she started scouring her mind for reasons to feel the hate, but there was nothing to latch on to.

That's when she began spontaneously noticing positive qualities in the woman's demeanor. She dressed nicely. She was helpful. Her tone wasn't so condescending as much as it was prudent. Janice realized that she had been taking things personally that were never personal. The woman wasn't so bad after all. They ended up having a wonderfully genuine interaction, and Janice discovered that the woman actually admired her and her work. This not only strengthened their professional bond but led to the promise of a new friendship. Janice had been lifted out of an old, outdated, and possibly unfair perspective and could now give this relationship another chance.

Janice came to meditation because she wanted to sleep better, but—as always—its benefits wound up spilling over into her waking hours.

COPING WITH THE UNTHINKABLE

Meditation can help us become less rigid and more open to hope and possibility, even after enduring great sadness and disappointment.

My student Charlie is a college professor who teaches swing dancing on the side. I mention the swing instruction because Charlie has learned to embrace the more lighthearted side of life, a fact that is quite remarkable given what he lived with for many years.

When Charlie was young, his older brother committed suicide after a traumatic breakup. Since that day, Charlie always blamed his brother for what he did to their family. The words that he associated with his late brother were "coward," "weak," and "selfish," and he promised himself to never be like him. In fact, he usually just told people he was an only child in order to avoid talking about it. Charlie accepts that his brother's death deeply affected him and influenced many of his choices, but now he credits his six years of consistent meditation and therapy for helping him see his brother in a different light. Here is his report from the field:

> Meditation did two important things in reforming my relationship with my brother. First, it allowed me to see the relationship between cause and effect. It used to be that when I started to feel vulnerable in a relationship, I would run. I never wanted to get to that place where [my brother] was before he died. It took me a long time to see what was going on there, to recognize where that behavior was coming from.
>
> The other thing that meditation gave me was a glimpse of what's on the other side of all these problems I face. If I think that life is hard, rough, and painful, what's the point of fixing anything, since there's always going to be something that will go wrong. But through meditating I started to believe that being happy is a possibility and something I can choose. If that idea is true, then the sooner I start to deal with things I've neglected the sooner I can be happy.
>
> Meditation didn't solve all my problems magically, trust me—I still have plenty on the to-do list. But it loosened this figurative knot in my life so I could choose to start to untie myself. I know that without it, I wouldn't have started to do the work that needed to be done.
>
> I've noticed I don't get bothered when I hear about good things happening to others. When I used to hear of

the newest whiz kid to become a billionaire by inventing some fabulous thing I'd always think, "Why didn't I do that?" or "What's wrong with me? That person has it all figured out, why don't I?" Or I'd feel secretly happy when something didn't work out for somebody else. Meditation helped me understand that when I try and tear somebody down, including myself, it hurts me.

"Am I smart enough? Funny enough? What does so and so think about me?" I really used to worry about things like that. Then one day, a few months after I started to meditate, I came out of what I thought had been a crappy meditation, but something had happened. It was like I was waking up, very calmly, and realizing that worries like that are pointless. I can love and be loved, and no matter what happens to me ever, I'm still going to be fine. That there's no point to ever worry about anything, it's absolutely useless. That no-worries-ever-again feeling lasted about ten seconds, at most, but I can still remember it. If I have to meditate the next fifty years to have that experience once more, I'll happily do so.

For some reason, I decided to not meditate for a few days, just to see what would happen. By the first day I felt a little off, second day more off, during the third day while I was in traffic I started cursing at all the cars I could see. The weird thing was that nobody had cut me off or honked their horn at me; nothing had happened. I just felt anxious, angry, and small. It was exactly how I used to feel when I worked a job I hated after graduating from school. I don't experiment like that anymore.

—Charlie

THE COUPLE'S FIGHT GONE *RIGHT*

This real-life relationship story is one of my favorite examples of what it means to become more adaptable as a meditator, because at one time or another we've all been there.

Lori worked as a lawyer in New York. She had a very type-A personality, and was feeling the increasing pressure of work when she searched for a meditation teacher online and found my training. She showed up, admitted openly that she was a skeptic, but committed to learn anyway because she said she felt a genuine connection with me and trusted that I would lead her out of the valley of stress and into the promised land of rest, so to speak.

Cut to a year later, Lori returns to audit my training, and I'm sitting in a group of about fifteen meditators-in-training, teaching them about how stress release can cause the mind to become active in meditation. At this point, Lori fangs into me, saying that she's been meditating diligently for over a year and hasn't missed more than a handful of meditations, but it seems as though her practice has stalled. As I'm listening to her report, it sounds normal to me—she's simply experiencing a meditation plateau. But I let her continue to vent. She complained that she wasn't getting deep anymore, and that her mind was full of work concerns in "almost every meditation." She said she'd begun doubting the process, and to top it off, she claimed that her life hadn't really changed "all that much"—aside from getting marginally better sleep. But work was still just as stressful, and so on.

Where was this life-changing breakthrough? she wondered out loud. Where were all the improvements and benefits she'd been sold?

I told her that in a case like hers, where she had so much going on, I had no doubt that she was transforming. Aside from that, I reminded the entire group, it's not a good idea to gauge progress solely by what's happening *inside* of the meditation. And furthermore, it's just not possible to meditate more than seven hundred times and not receive at least some benefit. I assured Lori that what would probably happen was that someone else would see the transformation in her before she did.

About six months later, she sent me an email apologizing for being so aggressive with me that night when she sat in on the class. And then she relayed the following story:

As you know, I have been quite the skeptic, but I have something funny to tell you. Last time we met, you said that one day we will notice a change in our stress reactions or that someone else may notice it before we do. Well, about two weeks ago I was out to dinner with my husband. We had an argument for a few minutes (I was right, he was wrong—the usual). Then I sort of got over it and moved on and didn't think anything of it. About twenty minutes later, after he was sure the argument was dead and buried, he said, "You know, three months ago you would have walked out of the restaurant after that discussion and now you just let it go. I don't know if that's the meditation or what."

Okay, so *maybe* you are on to something.

—*Lori*

SUPER SUNDAY

Here's one more story of how real people show up when they're becoming more adaptable as a result of daily meditation:

Justin never intended to learn how to meditate. He only came to my training in New York because his wife, who had struggled with insomnia for years, took my course and immediately began sleeping better at night, along with other noticeable benefits. The next week, Justin—also an insomniac—was sitting in my course.

Some course participants ask a lot of questions and engage with the others around their shared experiences. But Justin was the quiet, observant type. He fit the profile of a "nice" skeptic. In other words, I could tell that he was doubtful, either about many of my claims or about his ability to benefit from meditation—but he was careful not to show it. During our third session, which fell on a Monday, Justin was unusually excited to share his experience from the night before.

Justin and his family had traveled to his sister-in-law's house on Long Island for dinner, as they all did every Sunday evening—it had become a family tradition. The problem was that Justin didn't get along with his sister-in-law (to put it politely), but he reluctantly went to the weekly dinner because it was important to his wife, and he wanted to keep the peace at home. He also knew deep down that his frustration with his sister-in-law was somewhat irrational. The agreement with his wife was that when they arrived at her sister's house, he would announce to everyone that he had an early morning the next day and therefore they had to leave right after the meal.

On this occasion, Justin made his usual announcement, but for some reason he found himself lingering at the table for an extra half hour. The adults moved to the living room while the kids played, and then a full hour went by and he realized he was still enjoying himself. Then another hour passed, and he didn't even notice. Before long, it was midnight, the kids were passed out, and Justin's wife was standing by the door with the baby asleep in her arms, persuading *him* to leave. It was the most bizarre thing, he reported, because the usual discontent he would feel at their Sunday evening gatherings had completely evaporated and been replaced with joy. Everything on the surface was the same (same house, same sister-in-law, same night of the week). But there was a new and improved Justin.

A capacity to tolerate someone whom we find annoying is a less powerful skill than cultivating an ability to find enjoyment at almost any time, in almost *any* setting—but that was what Justin had achieved after two days of meditating. This skill is what you're cultivating each time you remain E.A.S.Y. and treat all thoughts passively. It's not possible to have a passive attitude in meditation and not have it carry over into your life *outside* of meditation. It's a direct by-product of inner change, and meditation is the catalyst for that change.

13

RETHINKING MINDFULNESS

Here's Sarah's report from the field, which beautifully captures the idea of mindfulness:

> Before I learned to meditate I read a book that talked about being present in everything you do, whether it be sweeping the floor, washing your car, or making a pot of coffee. And although I understood conceptually how important it was and could appreciate the sentiment, it was like a short fuse for me: as quickly as I would acknowledge the moment, it disappeared because of a chain of thoughts, an interruption, etc.
>
> But I was washing vegetables for a salad today, and was present to my hands washing the vegetables, the water beating down on them, and the shiny silver of the sink. I was in a state of calm appreciation. These moments of serenity

and joy in my daily doings are happening more often and for longer periods of time.

I felt a peaceful feeling of "I am here." I wasn't in the past thinking about what someone said or how I should have responded, nor in the future worrying will something come to pass. I am here. Such a simple statement with profound effect. Meditation is the catalyst for many of these moments. They are plentiful. And I am continuously grateful.

—*Sarah*

Mindfulness and meditation are often treated as interchangeable, but they are different. I actually see mindfulness as the *by-product* of daily meditation—the end result, not the means.

When we mistakenly make mindfulness the means (the technique), we risk becoming too preoccupied with so-called "mindful" activities as opposed to simply being present. Present moment awareness is not about singling out one thing or one sensation to pay attention to at a time. It's about being present to everything that the mind can organically and dynamically perceive. In other words, instead of being exclusive with our awareness by focusing on one or two things at a time, we want to allow inclusiveness and embrace the entire experience, from the surface to the subtle level.

Think of it like having a conversation. If you try to listen to one word at a time, or only to the sound of someone's voice as they are speaking, or only look at their eyes while speaking, you will miss a lot of crucial information. Mindful communication is multilayered. It's tone of voice, words, pauses, eye contact, body language, tempo, reading between the lines, and so much more. In other words, when you're *trying* to be mindful, it's forced, and there's no natural discrimination occurring.

For survival reasons, we are preprogrammed to attend to the most important sensory information in every moment. By overriding that function and unnaturally paying attention to less important information for the sake of trying to be "mindful," we may miss some important subtle cues that reveal future change.

One unfortunate example of the repercussions of missing cues happened on the morning of December 26, 2004, when a magnitude-9 earthquake triggered the massive tsunami that swept across the Indian Ocean, wreaking havoc on the coastlines of twelve countries and killing over 150,000 humans. But strangely, very few animals were reported dead.

According to eyewitnesses, about an hour before the tsunami struck, dogs refused to go outside, there were elephants calling out and running for higher ground, flamingos abandoned their low-lying breeding areas, and zoo animals hid in their enclosures and could not be enticed to come back out.

The belief is that animals, both domestic and wild, possess a sixth sense—a knowingness—that tips them off about future events. Some experts say that animals are so in tune with the earth's vibrations that they can detect impending danger long before it happens. When a human has this type of internal hunch and it's just a feeling, we call it our intuition. If it's more fully formed as a clear thought, then it becomes a cognition. Either way, we need to listen to it and, if necessary, take action. When we do, good things generally happen. When we ignore our internal hunches, we usually end up being victimized in some way.

I believe true mindfulness to be the precursor to intuition. It's about being so connected to the moment that we can sense impending danger or future success; we are able to "see around the corner." It's being able to hear the internal cues and nudges toward people, places, and things that are important for our personal growth and evolution. It's getting a hunch to call someone, and on the other end of the line, you hear, "Oh my God, I was just thinking about calling *you*." Sometimes we even refer to it as "divine intervention," "synchronicity," "serendipity," or an "inner calling." Those are all products of mindfulness—and very different from sitting around trying to taste the sweetness in the strawberry you're eating (that's more like focused awareness).

Mindfulness is a by-product of clearing away the barriers to your intuition, which are mainly your stress triggers. If old stress memories keep firing and yanking you back to the way you reacted to a similar situation a decade ago, they inhibit your ability to evolve in accordance with your present level of understanding about yourself and life in general.

As your stress-associated memories dissolve through repeated exposure to rest, you gradually become liberated, and you'll find yourself able to engage more fully in moments that may involve similar elements or people who triggered you in the past. Except you'll find yourself less worried about the future, rehearsing your past less often, and not sweating the small stuff as much. You may not even be aware that you're being fully present—which is actually the *highest* form of mindfulness.

If you have to be mindful of being mindful, then are you really that mindful? I don't think so. It's like the previous observation about using focus-based thinking to settle the mind in meditation—it's not possible. True mindfulness is being so engaged in the moment that you're not thinking about being in the moment at all. Consider the feelings associated with falling in love, or walking in nature and witnessing a sunset or a waterfall, or playing a sport that you're good at. In each of these experiences, it's easy to lose awareness of what you're doing—not because you don't care, but because you're *so* present that you automatically go beyond surface-level awareness and into more of a settled state, which is what you often hear referred to as "the zone." It's like meditation, except your eyes are open and you can continue taking everything in, and you feel more. Colors appear brighter. Sensations are heightened. Time appears to stand still. And the next thing you know, hours have passed in what felt like minutes. That's what true mindfulness feels like— a flow state.

The other, more pedestrian understanding of mindfulness often feels laborious, as you're sitting there fighting your busy surface mind while trying to pay attention to fragments of the present moment and ignoring all of the rest. It's an okay start, but there are richer experiences to be had.

Report from the Field: The Art of Surrendering

Tomorrow is my first anniversary of learning to meditate. What a whirlwind of change this year has been. This time last year I couldn't even imagine living one more day, and now, precisely because of that dark period, I am willing to follow my heart wherever it wants to lead me. Life is too short to stay within any confines. And because of a year of meditation I trust in the process of life. It is starting to take hold and I am much more aware now of the thoughts I think and their implication on divine process.

However, in meditation, I have also completely let go of the need to control what happens and I no longer care, or even notice much, if thoughts are present or not. I've also stopped journaling about the "quality" of each meditation, and roaming thoughts no longer control me in the way they used to.

Now I awake each day with a wonder of what is in store for me, with a deep sense of anticipation instead of dread, and a knowingness that change is good and when one opportunity has run its course there are still limitless others available to me.

My overall sense of well-being and fulfillment is the highest it has ever been. I smile easily and often. And someone at work recently mentioned that my face looked "softer."

—*Joanna*

TWO PATHS, ONE CHOICE

There are essentially two ways we can approach life: do more and accomplish less, or do less and accomplish more.

Most people are engaged in the first approach—doing more and accomplishing less. They don't know this, of course. All they know is that life is hard, bills are always due, breaks are few and far between, and there's no time for anything extracurricular that doesn't involve drinking, sex, or satisfying any of the other endless cravings of the body.

At first, the notion of doing less to accomplish more seems like an illusion. A fantasy. A line from *The Karate Kid*. But this is precisely what you can expect as you make the experience of settling your mind and body a non-negotiable priority twice each day.

Being mindful and present can transform otherwise mediocre life experiences into precious and memorable moments, rich with insight and information about what's really important. This will make you unflappable. And others will notice—not that it matters, because you become *less* concerned with what others think of you anyway, good or bad.

It's pretty easy to determine which approach you (or anyone) are currently engaged in, by the way: if life is constantly surprising and shocking you, and causing you to run around playing defense most of the time—you know, frantically putting out a seemingly endless number of financial, emotional, and physical fires—you are most likely engaged in the do-more-to-accomplish-less approach.

Conversely, if you seem to be in the flow of life, are able to adapt as needed, and can see change coming from miles away—so that you have time to reorient yourself to take advantage of the flow instead of getting knocked off balance by its force—then you are most likely engaged in the do-less-to-accomplish-more approach.

No matter where you are, refinement is always in order. Do less to accomplish more, do least to accomplish most. And when possible, do "nothing" and accomplish "everything." Doing nothing doesn't mean sitting on your hands waiting for things to happen. It means doing what feels most natural while completely surrendering to the end result, knowing that you can never go wrong if your intentions are pure and your thoughts, words, and actions are no longer being dictated by your body's stresses.

This is what enjoying meditation does. It creates ultimate freedom within. And this is bliss.

YOUR MISSION

Now that you have the meditation technique, reminders, analogies, and a host of real-life stories from the field, I want to circle back to the goal of meditation, because I know from experience how easy it is to become so overwhelmed by thinking about all of the principles that you lose sight of the simple goal, which is to be E.A.S.Y. Being E.A.S.Y. unlocks all of the power of meditation, and keeps it enjoyable in the process.

The way we measure success is the extent to which we're being easy while meditating. Therefore, a "successful" meditation is not one where you go deep or experience a settled mind, but rather one where you are E.A.S.Y. with your thoughts and all other experiences. Remember, a settled mind is the by-product of being E.A.S.Y., not the other way around.

I also want to encourage you to adopt new meanings for what most untrained meditators refer to as "good" and "bad" meditations. For you, let a "good meditation" mean one that you do. Period. And let a "bad" meditation mean one that you skip. So every meditation you make the time for moves the needle forward. Every one you skip halts progress.

If you happen to have an extremely thought-filled meditation, instead of calling it "bad," like amateur meditators, let's refer to that as an "unsatisfying" experience (I like this word because it describes the experience, and not the validity of the experience). Likewise, let's replace "good" with "satisfying": "That was a very satisfying meditation—my mind became very settled."

And finally, let's gauge progress *only* by our ability to adapt to change outside of meditation—not by the content of our thoughts during meditation. You will have some beautiful thoughts, and some incredibly bizarre thoughts. It doesn't matter. You've learned how to navigate them all sufficiently. The expert swimmer doesn't care what color the water is. If she can swim, she can move through it with efficiency.

At the end of my live trainings, I tell my students, "If you feel like this information is a lot to remember, don't worry—with practice it gets much easier. And soon it will become second nature."

I'll share one more story with you, about a time I felt overwhelmed. Before I moved to Los Angeles, I planned to come for a month-long visit, and a good friend of mine was generous enough to loan me his car during my stay. He happened to be out of town when I arrived at the airport, so he arranged to have one of his neighbors meet me at the airport terminal with the car to hand me the keys. This happened without a hitch. Then his neighbor got into the car of a buddy who had followed him to the airport to give him a lift elsewhere and headed off, leaving me curbside with my friend's car, his keys, and my luggage.

As I loaded my luggage into the trunk of the car, and then sat in the driver's seat, I discovered that my friend had a manual transmission. I'd been assuming it would be an automatic. This was a big problem. Aside from watching other people drive stick-shift cars, I'd never actually driven one myself. I sort of knew conceptually what needed to happen—press my foot on the clutch, and then the gas, then shift gears, or was it the other way around? Uh-oh, I thought. And remember, I was still at the airport. Curbside. And this was just after the terrorist attack on September 11, 2001—before smartphones and ride-sharing services, but during the height of airport security officers blowing their whistles incessantly and threatening to issue me a ticket if I didn't move along.

Needless to say, I stalled countless times en route to where I was staying, and it was as embarrassing and miserable as you can imagine. But after a week, I started getting the hang of it. Having no choice but to learn made a big difference. Los Angeles is a car town, and I had to drive nearly everywhere. By the end of my stay, my gear-shifting became so smooth that it felt like I was driving an automatic.

So trust me, I know what it's like to be handed the keys to something and feel overwhelmed as I try to figure it out. If anything about meditation feels like that to you, just think of it like learning to drive a stick shift. At first you may be preoccupied with five or six concerns at once, and you will certainly feel like your practice is stalling and jumpy. But with daily practice, you'll be surprised by how, after not even a week or two of consistency, meditation will feel more and more natural. A month into your practice, meditation will start to become second nature. And a year after that, you'll wonder how you ever got through life without meditation.

Some experts claim that people can't learn meditation from a book, but I hope you feel inspired enough to prove them wrong. The big advantage of learning from this book is that you can refer back to it over and over. When I teach my live courses, the knowledge is given orally, and while there is plenty of practice, people often forget the details and nuances. So I have to remind them again and again. But you have it all in your hands right now, and you are free to continue reviewing these principles until you understand them inside and out.

And finally, I want to remind you of the larger purpose of making time to meditate daily. No matter how we slice it, the world needs more blissful people in it, and fewer people who are suffering unnecessarily. Unfortunately, some suffering in certain parts of the world can't be avoided. But if we don't have bombs raining down on us, and if we're not directly affected by political corruption, famine, or a natural disaster, then we don't have the right to suffer (particularly unless we've exhausted all options, like meditation), because we can't suffer in isolation; our suffering contributes to that of others.

The great news is once you feel happier, you'll find that it's not possible to be happy in isolation, either. Others will feel uplifted by your internal state of happiness, cultivated and eventually stabilized through meditation.

However we feel inside will be reflected in our perception of the world. Our responsibility as human beings is to make sure we're generating as much balance and bliss within ourselves as possible, so that we can continue sending more happiness, acceptance, and gratitude out into the world. If we want a green forest, the majority of the trees must be green. Likewise, if we desire to live in a peaceful world, the people must be peaceful. In other words, we are each personally responsible for doing our part, each day, to help cultivate the type of world that we want. And now you have a daily action step for creating peace within.

I wish you well on your journey. Send news of your meditation adventures and benefits, expected and unexpected, to blissmore.co, and let's continue to share our stories with others so together we can inspire more people to partake in and benefit from this simple practice. Godspeed, and happy meditating.

ACKNOWLEDGMENTS

I'm eternally grateful to my parents, Donald and DeAndra, for your unwavering love and support. You both kept me smiling and laughing my entire life, and in the process you've taught me how to lead with honesty, to go out of my way to help others, and, above all, to stay curious.

I thank each of my siblings, nieces, and nephews. You inspire me to think differently, and I always feel recharged after spending time together.

To Bryndan, Jonni, Matt, and Will, your friendship and counsel have meant more to me than you will ever know. I appreciate your patient ear and your words of wisdom.

A special thanks to The Shine team (Ali, Alison, Andrea, Anthony, Dave, Megan, Nuzi, and Olympia) for your encouragement and support while writing, as well as to Agapi, Alexi, Amely, Dhru, Guru Jagat, Kaya, Kute, Leon, Lewis, Mallika, Neil, Preston, and Suze for sharing your publishing experiences with me during my process.

I want to thank you, Dana, for introducing me to Coleen. Coleen, I feel so fortunate to have you as my agent. You've had my back since day one, and you've been so instrumental in helping me shape my initial vision for *Bliss More*, and for guiding me through the world of publishing.

Thank you, Becky, my right-hand editor, for your encouragement while I found my writing voice, and for patiently mentoring me throughout the writing process. Thank you also for helping to mold my thoughts and words into the final manuscript, and for helping to bring them to life.

Also thank you to my Ballantine editor, Marnie, for shepherding me through each draft, for your deadlines, your sage guidance, and timely suggestions (especially when you suggested that I re-write the book after handing it in the first time). Your patience, insight, expertise, and genuine interest in understanding meditation truly helped *Bliss More* evolve into a book that we're all very proud of, and I'm forever grateful that you shared my vision from the beginning.

I'd also like to thank the wonderful Ballantine team, namely Kara, Kim, Jennifer, Betsy, Christine, Andrea, Nancy, Marietta, and Maggie. Each of you has proven how amazing the publishing process can be when you have a powerful team backing you.

A very special thanks to Dr. Benson for generously taking time to speak with me about your extensive research and personal experiences in the early days of meditation research. I'd also like to acknowledge Dr. Davidson's lab for answering my many questions about their research.

Thank you to my beloved guru, MVS, who first introduced me to the easiest way of meditating I've ever known, and for teaching me by example how to connect with my students, and how to teach with grace, humor, and humility. Thank you to your teacher, to his teacher, and to all of the teachers of the tradition who have taken great care to pass the ancient meditation principles down in their purity over thousands of years.

Thanks to my meditation teacher colleagues—Ben, Charlie, Christopher, Gary, James, Jeff, Jill, Jillian, Laura, Michael, Robert, Theo, Tim, Yashoda, and the rest—who have been in the trenches with me over the years, always willing to leap into action in order to help the householders of the world become self-sufficient meditators.

I want to extend eternal gratitude to all of my meditation students. Every time I have had the honor of going on the teaching journey with you, I come out on the other end a better teacher for it.

A special thanks to those students who allowed me to reprint your stories and field reports in the pages of this book. Reading about your personal experiences is as important to the process of learning as understanding the principles of meditation, and your stories will undoubtedly inspire countless readers to begin and stay consistent in their daily meditation practice.

Thanks to the staff at Zinque who generously refilled hundreds of glasses of iced tea for me while I was writing the majority of this book.

And, finally, thank you to life, for being my greatest teacher and for always providing me with everything I need.

INDEX

meditation (*cont'd*):
  types of, xvi
  yoga and, xxiii; *see also* yoga
    classes; yoga teachers
meditation altars, 20
meditation basics, 6–8
  see also meditation technique
meditation benefits, 115–215
  adaptability and, 191–203
  cognitions and, 175–90
  effectiveness and, 115–28
  medication vs., 158–74
  mindfulness and, 204–15
  sleep effect and, 129–37
  stress release and, 138–57
meditation books, xxvii, xxxi, 133,
  214
meditation communities, 104,
  115–16
meditation effectiveness:
  measuring progress and,
    118–20, 194, 212
  pop culture claims and,
    115–18
  relaxation response and,
    122–28
  white coat phenomenon and,
    120–22
meditation fundamentals, *see*
  meditation position
meditation glow, xx, 135
meditation journals, 104
meditation plateaus, 185–88,
  199

meditation position, xiv, xvi, xx, 9,
  13–19, 80, 83, 108–9, 179
meditation purposes, xxii, 37–38,
  115–28
  see also meditation benefits
meditation schedule, xxx, 3, 54,
  85, 107–8
meditation setting, xxxi, 20–22,
  27, 103–4, 159–62, 171
meditation students:
  Amber, 136
  Charlie, 196–99
  Cole, 162–67, 172
  Franklin, 153–54
  George, 162–72
  Harriet, 175–77
  Janice, 195–96
  Jennifer, 192–94
  Johnny, 158–63
  Justin, 201–3
  Lori, 199–201
  Mona, 150–52
  Otto, 131–35
  Vicki, 136–37
meditation studies, 115–22
meditation teachers, xix–xxii, MV,
  13, 87–88
  breathwork and, 106
  Martha, 14–15
  social media and, 115
  teacher-student relationships
    and, 95–96
  traditional meditation and,
    34–36

ABOUT THE AUTHOR

Light Watkins has been practicing and teaching meditation since the late 1990s. In addition to reaching tens of thousands through his classes—private, public, and online—he enjoys producing meditation content for wellness communities such as mindbodygreen and Wanderlust. Light is also the founder of The Shine Movement, a popular live variety show that features meditation, music, film, inspirational storytelling, and philanthropy, with events all over the world. Watkins continues to speak and lead international meditation retreats and trainings.

blissmore.co

lightwatkins.com

theshinemovement.org

Facebook.com/lightw1

Twitter: @LightWatkins

Instagram: @lightwatkins

ABOUT THE TYPE

This book was set in Garamond, a typeface originally designed by the Parisian type cutter Claude Garamond (c. 1500–61). This version of Garamond was modeled on a 1592 specimen sheet from the Egenolff-Berner foundry, which was produced from types assumed to have been brought to Frankfurt by the punch cutter Jacques Sabon (c. 1520–80).

Claude Garamond's distinguished romans and italics first appeared in *Opera Ciceronis* in 1543–44. The Garamond types are clear, open, and elegant.